Face Depression Bravely

Mental Self-help Notes For Patients with Major Depression

By Gary Xing

Face Depression Bravely

-- Mental Self-help Notes for

Patients with Major Depression

(This book does not contain real names and places other than the authors and their works cited in this book. Any similarity is purely coincidental.)

There are no real people here,

There are no real events.

There are only real dilemmas,

And real struggles.

Preface

Depression is a very terrible psychological disease, even a "psychological cancer" said. Even people who study mental illness can't fully understand the horror of depression if they don't have it. Japan's famous series of horror film "the monstrous new ear bag," there was a story, about a young office worker called zhe also suffers from severe depression, can no longer bear any pressure, but his love, but do not understand it, just when he was depressed and helpless blindly encouraged him to go to work and make them a happy life, this has become the final pressure of crushing him down. Tetsuya eventually hangs himself, and his dead spirit drags his neck as he returns home late at night to visit his lover, which becomes the most terrifying scene in the episode. At the end of the story, Tetsuya's lover finally understands that for people suffering from severe depression, all warm encouragement is like a knife into the heart. But when we look at it from the perspective of a depressed person, we will discover a more frightening fact: they can not withstand mild stress, sometimes even can not withstand sincere care, just like a starving person walking in a desert full of thorns, the heart is full of despair, but do not know where to go. And healthy people who don't know about depression may look at these mentally ill people as if they were freaks.

It's enough to make a normal person depressed,

but it is.

I used to be a major depressive disorder patients, because before adulthood has been in the family violence environment, so the symptoms of depression from when I was a teenager has been presented, but then I don't know what happened, don't know what you're into the state, of course, more do not know oneself are already suffering from mental illness.

In China, the general awareness of mental illness is very poor, people do not know the difference between psychological illness and neurological disease, and it is very ignorant to taboo these mental problems. Whether it's depression, anxiety, obsessive-compulsive disorder, bipolar disorder, etc., it's all called psychopathy and used as a swear word. In the 21st century, this is still the case in mainland China. Imagine that thirty years ago, when I was young, who would have bothered to pay the medical bills for a stupid little boy who didn't talk and didn't laugh? Kind people would say that the child is introverted. Other people will say that this child is rather devious, wooden, stupid, do not know who, but in a word, it is normal.

Fortunately, perhaps because of God's mercy, or because of my extraordinary tenacity of life, I was fortunate enough to find some psychological adjustment methods, and then accidentally realized self-rescue. Even now, as a middle-aged man, I often inadvertently fall into that depressed and painful state of mind. I was tested using the international standard SDS psychological self-assessment form for depression, and the results showed that I was still a major depressive disorder. The recurring entanglement of the disease is evident. I have friends who I know have this problem. We all need some way to help ourselves psychologically.

Why must do psychology help oneself?

I'm not an anti-medical maverick, I'm just saying that if you're in the mood to go to the hospital, maybe you're not truly suffering from major depression. On the other hand, I'm really not sure if someone with major depression is in the mood to search and read this book. But I still believe that this is the most important value of this self-help notebook, as long as you have a little bit of hope in your heart, we can work together to create a fire of hope.

I'm not a psychology professional, I'm not a medical professional, I'm just an ordinary patient. I don't know whether this disease can be cured or not. I just share my self-help methods and continue to complete self-help by writing down notes. I hope and encourage patients who have conditions to go to regular hospitals for professional treatment and assistance. But for those who don't have medical or financial conditions, or for some reason can't take this step, let's face depression bravely and finally help ourselves.

(Plus: The Ultimate Way to Help Yourself - Find someone you can truly trust and confide your scariest secrets from your deep heart. A word of caution: don't try this, because you could go really crazy unless you find someone you can really trust.)

About Author

Gary Xing is a poet and author of fiction. He is the author of a collection of poems, *Trace of Time*, *Letters to the Future*, horror novels, *Strange Stories of A Stranger,* and a collection of photos *Tianjin, the City Where I Used to Live*. You can find other works by searching "Gary Xing, Guangyue Xing" on Amazon.

Let's start searching today!

Contents

Ⅰ·**What is Depression Disorder**

For the definition of "depression", I chose a relatively objective and popular introduction from Wikipedia, which reads as follows.

Depressive disorder (D), often referred to as depression or melancholia, is an emotional disorder characterized by Depressive mood. It mainly includes: major depression, persistent depression, seasonal depression. The common symptoms are: prolonged depression that is significantly more than necessary, lack of confidence, avoidance of people, even guilt, a marked decrease in energy, a reduced sense of time, and an inability to experience pleasure in any activity. This kind of disorder can also cause the patient's physical dysfunction, such as sleep disturbance or appetite increase or decrease, pain and so on."Depression" (from wikipedia entry: https://zh.wikipedia.org/wiki/%E6%86%82%E9%AC% B1%E6%80%A7%E7%96%BE%E6%82%A3).

Depression, like many other diseases, can lead to multiple complications. From the perspective of patients, most of these complications are mental, while a few directly affect the functional organs and humoral elements of the body. For example, depression will affect and reduce the serum concentration in the brain of patients, resulting in persistent fatigue, decreased appetite, sleep disorders and so on. From a healthy person's point of view, depressed people on the whole are not particularly different from healthy people, perhaps just look a little lazy, sluggish, dispiriting. But from the patient's point of view, if compared with the mental pain, the physical change is only a minor effect.

From my own feelings, the mental impact of depression is not simply pathologic depression, it can be counted as a mental attack. This attack is self-inflicted, multifaceted and multimental, and the results are horrific. If the depressed patients themselves are not aware of this mental level under attack, the probability of being easily defeated by depression is very high. It may be hard for people to realize that their soul is attacking them, but depression is just that. Because you can't see the enemy in the real world, and it's hard to realize from a third party that you're under attack, you can't organize effective mental resistance, and depression wins easily.

After the victory of depression, the patient's spirit will fall into a state of breakdown of different degrees, some slight, some serious, but the mental pain is difficult to avoid. Most of the time, even without the sufferer knowing it, his or her own mental state has been plunged into the terror space of major depression. Patients with mental pain and depression, it is difficult to help, and the health people around them are difficult to identify the patient's state, thought that it is just ordinary because of the difficulties in the world and the heart is sad, introverted and do not love to talk, even if the patient has a good relationship with friends, perhaps also just a few words of comfort, and then continue their own lives. All of this is normal, no problem, until the depressed person finally gets over the painful psychological process, or finally takes his own life.

II·Observe Depression from Multiple Angles

In The 2017 British horror film Ghost Stories, The main character reiterates the idea that "The brain sees what it wants to see." I think so. People often think they see the real world, but that's not necessarily the way it is. When it comes to depression, even in the same cubicle, a depressed person sees things very differently from a healthy person. This also makes it difficult for people with depression to help themselves, and difficult for healthy people to help. And because of the difference in perspective and feeling, people may even think that they are hurting each other, which makes the situation worse.

The stories listed in this book, partly from my own psychological experience, partly from my observation and understanding of the real experience of patients around me, I will show what depression is like from the perspective of both healthy people and patients with depression. Although these stories are based on real life, the names of the people and places in the stories are not real. The point is perspective and feeling, not who they are.

There are several characters in the book, but maybe they are all the same person, and this is not a joke. If you don't understand this, congratulations, you are healthy in terms of the subject matter of depression. Of course, everyone is unhappy sometimes. However, if you find yourself with a friend or colleague who has been exhibiting any of the special behaviors or abnormalities described in the story for many days, as a healthy person, please do your best to gently help them, at all costs.

If you are already suffering from depression, I think it will be helpful for you to have a look at the perspective of a healthy person. What you think is bad about yourself may not be the same for others. Of course, what you think is good for you may not be good for others. In short, try to see the wider world.

Now, let's look at the stories.

Feeling 1) Feeling Extremely Depressed

At 6 a.m., before the alarm clock sounded, Allen himself opened his eyes.

Over the years, he has developed a very effective internal clock. Like setting an alarm clock on yourself, mentally tell yourself what time you are going to wake up the next morning and you will wake up at that time, often a few minutes earlier.

At the beginning of his career, Allen was full of enthusiasm for struggle. He took on heavy work assignments, often going to bed at 12 PM and getting up at 4 am to continue working. Those eight hours outside of work could have been spent enjoying life or getting paid for working overtime. However, there was no such system and atmosphere in the general social environment, and Allen himself did not think it was a bad thing. Young people should be full of passion for struggle and drive for career, and the sense of fullness of less sleep and more work was like a drug that made Allen addicted. Allen never wanted to get rich or get promoted. He never did anything like gifts or bribes. He simply believed that work should be selfless, hard-working, conscientious, down-to-earth, and ultimately effective. After four years of such struggle, he unexpectedly achieved a small success in his career, and became the youngest management cadre in the enterprise, that is, the head of the department in which he worked.

Although the work and life did not change much, but then things began to be a little different.

First Allen's body began to struggle. Long hours of office paperwork had chained Allen's body, leaving him no extra time for exercise. Allen didn't even bother to exercise for work. In addition, the drinking culture of the workplace had taken a toll on Allen's liver, spleen and stomach. As a result, he became overweight, had a fatty liver, elevated blood lipids, lost exercise endurance, and even had weaker arms. Only the fingers seem to have retained their original strength and become more flexible.

Second, colleagues and friends begin to fall apart. Allen was originally the youngest member of the department, but because of his hard work, he became the department leader directly, which made the senior employees find it hard to accept. But the workplace is not a battlefield. People are here to make money and support their families. There is no need to fight it out. As a result, people tacitly isolated Allen and watched him act as a monologue with the attitude of watching jokes. The work Allen assigned, pretending to obey orders, was only perfunctory, almost floating in the air, with no progress at all. As the youngest department head, Allen was embarrassed to lose his temper with his subordinates, so he had to arrange work for himself and finish it by himself, completely becoming a lone Wolf.

Thirdly, in front of the superior leaders, even though Allen became the section chief, there was no special change in his status. He was just an ordinary worker. On the contrary, because he was promoted, he had to take on more responsibility and more blame than before. All this, Allen had to break his teeth to swallow, all had to bear it. Allen is not the kind of person who fawns on leaders, butters up to them, treats them and gives them gifts. He is also not the kind of person who has a strong backer and parachute into the world to enjoy his happiness. In the eyes of leaders, Allen is probably just a dog who can bark and bite better. Allen was vaguely aware of this, but he didn't dare or want to admit it.

Finally, Allen did not have the time and mood to fall in love, nor did he have the time and mood to take care of his parents and relatives. Under the banner of "dedication" and "struggle", he actively and passively separated himself from his own personal life. Few people volunteered to understand and care about Allen's feelings, because people of his age were basically going through similar things.

Allen's mood began to become depressed, depressed, lost the motivation to fight, every cell in his body felt tired. The tedious day after day of typing, talking on the phone, and doing errands even gave him the urge to hit someone. But Allen didn't even bother to lift his hand, and hitting someone was only a flash of imagination. Looking at the more than 20 tasks on the daily work list, each of which could not be completed in a day and half a day, and was pressed on his own body, the leader also asked him to complete it within a day, which made him feel a kind of bruise of brain blockage.

Allen sat up reluctantly in bed and pressed the off button of the alarm clock. The sky outside the window was still overcast.

A night's sleep did nothing to soothe Allen's weariness, which seeped through his body. He wanted to get rid of his daily to-do list and have a good rest. But what about "taking a break"? At this point, Allen couldn't even "relax". Apart from his busy work, he even forgot what life was like. There's a meeting for everyone in the department early in the morning, so don't think about it any more."Allen told himself.

The department Allen leads is not big. Although the personnel has been adjusted in recent years, the number of staff is still only four people, and each person has his own mind, which makes Allen a headache. He knew that even if the meeting was assigned, they would not do the work required. According to the current rules, once you become an employee in the enterprise, as long as you do not break the law or commit a crime, you will not be fired. Even if the work efficiency and quality are low, Allen's superior leader will not bother to find Allen's subordinate employees to hold them accountable, and Allen is the only one to be criticized. There were no incentives or punishments in the department, so Allen had nothing to do with them. Allen watched as the four men sat around eating breakfast, checking their phones, and painting their nails. They sullenly finished reading their schedules and then went their separate ways.

All day, Allen sat in front of his computer, his eyes glazed over, his expression numb, his fingers tapping away at the keyboard. Even when his subordinates asked, his voice was dull and feeble. He didn't care about the world. He just wanted to go home and get into bed.

Allen reports to four healthy people. Some were older than Allen, some were younger than Allen. No matter how old you are, you should not be careless about your job. But given this wonderful loophole in the system, it seems only natural to exploit it. They watched Allen change from an ordinary newcomer in the workplace 4 years ago to a department leader today, and they all knew very clearly that Allen was a hardworking person. However, in their opinion, Allen is rigid and inflexible. He only knows empty talk about "enduring hardship" and "selfless dedication". He only cares about himself when getting promoted and rich, but does not know how to seek benefits for others around him. Since Allen's earnest efforts have not brought him any real benefit and have even hindered his ascent, Allen's earnest efforts seem foolish and even evil to them. Recently, perhaps it is some kind of karma, Allen has become very silent, few words, the movement has become slow, the whole person seems to have become a fool. Fight for fame and fortune in the end, it serves you right.

It seems that the leader is not so easy to be. This is the view that the four staff members can agree on most.

Feeling 2) Loss of Self-worth: A Strong Sense of Inferiority

Winni is a freshman at Tianhe No. 3 High School. As a flower girl, she is full of expectations for the legendary high school life.

Winni likes reading very much. Since the second grade in junior high school, every weekend, she would go to the city library to look for books to read. At that time, she often listened to the senior students discussing the funny things in high school life together, such as the little red loves the little white, the little white loves the little flower, the Chinese teacher read out the strange wrong words, the poetry recitation club meeting, and so on. In Winni's mind, high school life is so colorful, 100 times better than her junior high school life.

But when Winni after hard work, finally admitted to everyone's envy of the city's key high school No. 3 Middle School, her mentality has undergone a huge change. The bright colors of high school were gone from her eyes, leaving only a gray, depressing scene.

In this key high school, talented people

everywhere, master cloud, Winni was proud of the literary expertise, but here is plain and ordinary. Students who are good at writing and reciting are everywhere. And many students' family economic environment is good, the dress is particularly outstanding, in wonderment, but also let Winni this simple used girl suddenly have a sense of shame. For the first time, she knew that young people could still dress up so smartly and look extraordinary even in their common school uniform. Looking at her appearance and figure like a dead branch, she experienced the feeling of inferiority deeply.

Maybe I don't deserve such a good school at all. A month into the semester, this sentence became a recurring one in Winni's mind.

Although everyone wears the same uniform, Winni deliberately pulls the collar a little higher, not to be trendy or unusual, but to cover her face. Even on days when she doesn't have to wear school uniform, she deliberately chooses dark clothes and shoes to hide behind the understated, almost transparent colors. Winni wants to make an effort to eliminate her existence.

At this age, girls become more conscious of their appearance and wear light makeup and simple accessories without breaking the school rules. Almost every girl will do this. But Winni is an exception. Her family was not rich, and the sense of "frugality" has been nailed into her personality. She longed to be pretty, and to try those sweet and delicate cosmetics, but in her mind even the wearing of a brightly coloured headdress made her think it was a sign of frivolity, and all her desires for beauty turned into repressed monsters in her heart. The budding of youth is a normal state of growth, so Winni's inner conflict became daily, intense, almost completely at a loss what to do. She felt that, dressed or not, she was a freak in the crowd, bound to be the object of ridicule. So she not only dressed low-key in the school, the act is away from the crowd, just want to stay alone, and will not say a word with others.

Winni wanted to fit in with the small class she had to face every day. But listening to the classmates around me every day to talk about the TV series, chat about the movie gossip, and can only recite the ancient prose of her for these trends but know nothing, she more feel like a zombie climb out of the grave, has been excluded from the modern civilization of the city thousands of miles away. Winni: What's more, I'm afraid that even though I study hard every day, my grades are at best average. And my classmates talk about entertainment news every day, but I still get excellent grades in all the tests. Winni couldn't understand, and the only answer she could think of was that she was a bum, a complete idiot. She couldn't even hold her head up because she was so depressed that she would wander around the campus with her head down every day between classes.

However, whose life does not grow in the struggle? Winni sometimes does the same for herself and tries to find ways to change herself. She began arriving at the classroom 30 minutes earlier each day, doing all the cleaning duties on her own, and even wiping down every desk. But instead of staying in the classroom and waiting for classes to begin, she would get out of the classroom as soon as she was done, then walk through the school's main entrance with the other students, pretending she had just arrived. She did not want her classmates to know that she was doing these things in secret, lest they say that the freaks were doing strange things. Two months later, the head teacher announced the first members of the class committee, and Winni was chosen as the class commissar in charge of life. Hearing the news, even she was taken aback.

Winni never thought she could be a member of the class committee. She had no idea what a life committee member was supposed to do. However, the members of the first class committee of each class are not elected by the students' votes, but chosen by the head teacher through observation, so that is to say, the teacher chooses himself. Winni didn't know for a long time that she didn't know what qualifications and abilities she had to take on the position of commissary in charge of life. So she summoned up her courage and went to the teacher's office to ask.

The head teacher Zhang Yamei is a kind and gentle woman, she explained to Winni: because Winni style is simple and practical, showed the good quality of hard work, so nominated her to become a member of the life, by example management and supervision of students to do a good job in daily health, to create a good learning environment. Zhang also said she could see that Winni was a very serious girl and believed that Winni would be able to finish the job. It is no exaggeration to say that this evaluation of Zhang teacher, Winni in her 16 years of life is the first time to hear for her positive affirmation and encouragement. Winni was very excited and grateful to Miss Zhang, but she could not accept this explanation, because she dared not. She wondered whether she could do the job well and whether she would betray the kindness of her teacher.

According to the duty requirements of the commissary in charge of life, Winni needs to arrange a health duty plan for each student in the class, specify the duty standard, and find the time to announce to the class. As Shakespeare wrote in The Merchant of Venice: Give him a rope to hang with, and for God's sake, nothing else! Winni's heart is to spend every day in this kind of suffering, and then drum up the courage, fight a life, to complete the task arranged by teacher Zhang. She didn't want to let Miss Zhang down. Even under the platform is the sound of the students laughing, she is still red face, loudly announced the duty arrangement.

This is definitely a good start, let Winni finally have a bit of courage to continue to change herself. Even though she still dresses modestly and hides from people, there seems to be something special about her behavior that makes Winni feel like she's not totally worthless.

In the second semester of her freshman year, Winni decided to sign up for a speech contest organized by the student union. The theme of the contest is "Protect the environment, cherish the earth", which is not a topic Winni is familiar with, but she is willing to try. In Winni's heart, in fact, always contains some kind of happy performance, happy to show the impulse. But with so much shame and disgust at even wearing a pink hairpin, it was almost hysterical to perform in public, and the impulse and talent was suppressed by herself. Now, that desire is reviving. Winni wanted to win the prize, so she looked through her research carefully. She wrote down four pages of her speech with pen stroke by stroke, and practiced secretly at home.

Because high school still focuses on exams, so these student activities are also simplified accordingly. There is only one opportunity for the speech contest at the school level, which is the preliminary, the semi-final and the final. The stadium is located in the student auditorium, which was originally narrow and seemed quite empty. Not many people attended. There were only five student judges, two or three students helping out, and about five students who competed. Winni sat in the back row away from the platform, in front of the speech, the heart is very nervous. Everyone seemed to be very casual, and the students were either standing on the platform and speaking seriously, or standing in front of the judges and saying what they wanted to say casually. The student judges were casual, too, and the question-and-answer session was almost like telling jokes. Winni: I don't like this situation. I think the game should be serious, and everyone should be very nervous, just like I am now. Nervousness and fear were normal, even though she didn't like it.

Finally it was Winni's turn to take the stage. She pinched her speeches, but decided to leave them on the table. She wants to play like a real speaker. But in reality, which is often cruel and funny, Winni underestimated the effects of nervousness and forgot all the words after saying "Hello everyone". She stood there, the lights shining down on her face, and the judges seemed to be sitting right in front of her, looking at her curiously as the air froze around her. One of the judges said, "Relax, just say something. Do you think we should protect the environment?""Yes," said Winni. Then there was silence again. She tried to find a beginning, but her blank mind could only produce a series of gibberish. A student staff member ran to the back and brought Winni's paper. Winni took the paper and realized that she might not even know the words. She picked up the sentences she could still make out and read them over, then hurried back to her seat from the stage. The whole game was like a strange dream. Winni looked at the four pages of blue and black pen-ink. She then rolled them into a paper ball and stuffed them into her mouth. It's hard and bitter. I almost choked to death when I swallowed it. It's just as well. You can save a rope to hang yourself.

Many years later, Winni bought a book of poetry, the name is "the track of time", there is a poem, accidentally cut into Winni's girlhood state of mind. The poem is called "inferiority complex" and it goes like this: inferiority complex is a strange dry well and you will never fall to the bottom.

Miss Zhang and Winni are surrounded by students who are physically and mentally healthy. In Miss Zhang's opinion, Winni is a hard-working and simple, serious and responsible girl. Her earnestness and responsibility are reflected in her ability to implement all aspects of the school regulations, such as wearing school uniforms, carrying school supplies, and finishing homework in good quality. Although she is introverted and somewhat isolated all the time, she has the desire to integrate into the collective in her heart. No matter whether there is morning class or not, Miss Zhang, as a head teacher, comes to school early every day. She herself is a very responsible and excellent teacher. By chance, she noticed Winni doing the cleaning alone in the early morning. After several days of observation, Miss Zhang was sure that Winni was doing it on purpose. It is because of Miss Zhang's kindness and delicacy that she did not explain this matter directly to the students, but gave Winni a chance to grow up. Becoming a member of the life committee, for students with physical and mental health, may only be a responsibility, and may even be a chore, but for Winni such a little inferiority, repressed the heart of the girl, is a very precious opportunity. As long as Winni grasps this opportunity, she can break through the siege of the heart and become a healthy child again. In a way, Winni did not live up to Zhang's expectations. She broke through her own limitations, though not completely. However, the process of growth is always long and hard, as long as we can take this step.

And in the eyes of the students who are physically and mentally healthy, Winni is absolutely a freak. Skinny and dry doesn't even begin to describe the eerie atmosphere surrounding Winni. As long as stay in Winni side, there will be an invisible sense of oppression, even loud talk has become very uncomfortable, let a person just want to hide away. Never mind being silent, but the way she looked at people was often strange, as if with some sort of anger or disdain. Not many people care about what everyone else is wearing -- after all, the school's uniform is mandatory -- but Winni seems to care enough about it to make everyone around her have a more nuance about what they're wearing. Of course, we hope that their appearance has some unique beautiful attributes, but also try to avoid in front of Winni show, several times over, we will always have a very strange feeling in the face of Winni.

This is not a problem for students who are physically and mentally healthy. After all, no one is a natural psychologist. Besides, you have to face and solve your own problems by yourself. Isn't it stupid and selfish to complain that others don't take the initiative to take care of you? Unfortunately, the reality is often so, each perspective is different, eventually to the formation of disaster.

Feeling 3) Meaningless: Losing Your Hobbies

Claude sat at home drinking beer. He lolled on the sofa, beer down his throat more easily than water.

In addition to the beer, vodka, rum, whiskey, ouzo and gin were arranged on a small table in front of him, almost like a wine tasting. In addition to alcohol, there were cigarettes on the side tables, but there were no dishes to serve alcohol or the sweet fizzy drinks used to make cocktails. For Claude, to make alcohol less stimulating was to desecrate it.

The soap opera on the television was Claude's only drink.

Claude had a decent job as a warehouse keeper in a car assembly plant. Because the factory is so profitable, the warehouse is always full of all kinds of parts. Claude is very busy every day, receiving goods, numbering, stacking and taking materials according to the requirements of the production line. An interesting feature of modern warehouse management, however, is that the maximum amount of work can be achieved by employing a very small number of people. In this factory, Claude can do all the warehousing work of the day shift by himself, so he seldom sees his colleagues.

During his long working hours, the whole world seemed like a closed, mechanized space, with no one to speak to and no sound beyond the running of the machines. Then suddenly one day, he was overwhelmed by a great sense of loneliness. This loneliness did not directly affect Claude's working state, but it destroyed his mood to some extent. Claude used to smoke a cigarette every five hours during his break. Now he needs to smoke one every hour. The work used to be happy and fulfilling, but now it is full of irritability.

He didn't know what was happening to him, but he couldn't get rid of his inner turmoil. He doesn't even know what he wants, because the job is no different. He was over forty years old, but he felt as if he had gone back to adolescence, with no extra desires in his body, but restless and restless in his heart. When this irritation builds to a climax, he even punches the stainless-steel shelves.

If this loneliness is a consequence of the lack of communication with others, then when the company holds an annual meeting or some kind of group meeting, although Claude and his colleagues sit together and can talk to each other normally, these things only aggravate his loneliness. Other than "hello" and "how are you?" he doesn't whisper about things in the company like his colleagues in other departments do. The warehouse is like an island in the company. No new information is generated. Even the noise of the wind is rare.

He began to think about his work and life, and felt that what he had done was useless and meaningless. If the company would spend money, he could replace himself with a more advanced intelligent robot, and this day would come sooner or later but surely.

Make no sense.

Claude spent a lot of time feeling this saying, he found that it seems to be applicable to any place in life.

Like Claude's interest. He was an avid shooter, and his interest in all types of firearms bordered on obsession. He obtained a legal gun license and bought several handguns, shotguns and rifles in consideration of his financial situation. He also had fun with the selection of ammunition, and he would exchange ideas with people in the shooting club. He even set up a small fund for himself to save up for the golden desert eagle pistol he had long wanted. But when his mind changed, he suddenly felt that these were very boring behavior, shooting on the shooting range could not bring him anything substantial, and the 25 yard indoor shooting range that used to be full of fun also seemed extremely narrow and short. Apart from wasting money and listening to a few sounds, shooting is nothing more than this. He's not going to be a legendary ranger in a western movie, and he's not going to be the kind of Wild Man he loves for a long time. It's just a boring fantasy. Make no sense.

At the same time as the love of shooting has lost its meaning, so has football. Claude was also a football fanatic, whether it is the "World Cup" or "Super Bowl", he tried to do everything not to miss the live game. Even just listening to the radio, the loud cheers set fire to every cell in his body. But when his mood began to change, the words "meaningless" were like a desert wind that swept away the enthusiasm in him. He even wondered why he had been so interested in watching humans chase a ball. In a limited amount of time, the players are frantically trying to grab the ball and try to get it into the net of the other team. They are very tenacious and very hard. But then what? Nothing special happened. The boring life goes on, the boring life is as usual, and nothing has changed in the world. It doesn't make any sense.

Even Claude's favorite pastimes became meaningless and uninteresting. Poker is just turning pieces of paper over and over. Chess is just moving small things around. Claude felt as if he had seen everything in the world, but he had not gained any new enlightenment. This insight may seem like some kind of illusion, but it is also meaningless.

The change in Claude's attitude was very sudden and rapid. Within a month, he was completely immersed in the world of wine. It seemed that only alcohol could numb and drive away this terrible loneliness and emptiness. He no longer carried out any activities based on hobbies and interests, on all the daily trivia is not interested, no longer shaving hair, personal hygiene is also done carelessly, the whole person seems to really become Robinson Crusoe. Unfortunately, he did not have Robinson's tenacious will and strong desire for life. To him, everything seemed meaningless, uninteresting, even gloomy and sad.

Claude works with people who are physically and mentally healthy. Although I don't usually see this chubby storekeeper, my overall impression of Claude is good. Careful and responsible, he has a flexible mind. He is very competent for the work requiring meticulous quality such as receiving goods and supplying materials, and he has always done a good job. However, I do not know what happened to him recently. When colleagues meet, Claude's words seem to have become less, and the overall temperament has become very depressed, which is different from the past. There was even a gray mist on his face, which I wonder if it was an illusion. At meetings with colleagues and the occasional lunch, Claude would talk about his gun, his marksmanship, which soccer stars were moving, what decorations he would wear in the Super Bowl, and there seemed to be no end to the conversation. But now he was lazy, lethargic, and seemed to be full of depression. If I got close enough, I could smell the alcohol all over him. Co-workers ask Claude if something is going on at home, but he doesn't bother to answer, because social etiquette prevents them from asking again. Claude's productivity was significantly slower, and although there was no mistake, the speed of supply and inventory clearing was significantly slower. The manager of the company also talked to Claude, but with nothing to show for it, he decided to give Claude some time off.

How would Claude find the time to buy so many drinks if he didn't rest?

Feeling 4) Unable to Feel Joy

Hogan works in an auto repair shop, where he is one of the oldest employees, with three apprentices. He has been in the auto repair industry for more than 30 years. No matter what kind of car, he can basically tell where the trouble is by listening to the engine sound. If the engine doesn't start, he has more than 20 simple methods to quickly detect the possible trouble. A car troubleshooter equipment is no longer a necessity for him. Even for the latest electric cars, he has a unique expertise in maintenance. What is more commendable is that he is more familiar with the maintenance of those ancient models of classic cars. These knowledge and experience are not what the young men who have just entered the line for a few years can fix, which is the gift from time. Due to his excellent skills in car repair and his enthusiasm and cheerful personality, Hogan has accumulated a large number of customer resources, and is respected by the owner of the car repair shop and his apprentices. His family is also very happy, two daughters have married, the eldest daughter is 4 months pregnant, is actively preparing everything to welcome this little life. Hogan is beaming as he prepares for the birth of the third generation of his family. He even thinks about what to call the baby. He had heard from his daughter that he was expecting a baby grandchild, so he thought it would sound better to call him Ron.

What a happy man this is. The more the accumulation of more powerful maintenance skills, will not be easily replaced by a stable career, respected workplace status, with a good relationship with customer groups, relatively easy daily work, enviable good income, healthy body and happy expectations. If you can get two or three of these things, life will be perfect. Hogan, on the other hand, owns it all. He's a happy man with a perfect life.

But things are not always as perfect as we expect. Hogan's eldest daughter was injured in a car accident while out shopping, but survived. But the baby she was carrying had already died.

When he heard the news, Hogan's legs gave way and he collapsed on the repair bench. He already knew and understood everything, but there was a kind of paste in his head that made him feel confused, and he seemed to have a hard time understanding what was happening. From this moment on, his state of mind changed significantly.

A major inner shock is inevitable, but what it looks like is no different from what it usually looks like. As an experienced maintenance technician, Hogan has weathered many difficulties in his career. He is not only brave in the face of difficulties, but also persevering. This time, he had survived the family disaster. He visited his daughter and offered his family spiritual and financial support. He also comforted his wife, who had supported and stood by him to this day. Hogan also received comfort from his family, but only he knew the results. Those consolations were sincere, but they did not soothe the pain he was suffering. He was especially looking forward to the arrival of the child and his transition from father to grandfather. But sadly, Laine died before he was born.

It is also a kind of separation.

In this case, Hogan experienced the pain of losing a loved one, the pain of giving away a black man, and the pain of losing the future he so eagerly anticipated. The multiple pain hits Hogan at the same time, making him look a lot older.

He didn't want to be decadent, and he knew very rationally that it was useless to dwell on pain. Soon after the accident, he returned to the garage and resumed his work.

Everything went on as usual, and the apprentices, well aware of the blow which the old gentleman had suffered, worked harder and harder, so as not to put any additional burden on him. Hogan knew the good will of the boys. He pretended to make a few offhand jokes as usual to liven up the atmosphere, but he couldn't say anything. There was something blocking his mind.

Customers came and went in an endless stream, everyone seemed relaxed and happy, and nothing in the world had particularly changed. But for some reason, people seemed to feel that there was something particularly dull about Hogan. On a hot summer day, the smell can even make people feel cold. Hogan knew what was happening to him, but there was nothing he could do to improve the situation. He knew he had psychological problems, but he couldn't fix them the way he could fix his car. He still smiled at each customer, tried to greet them warmly, and repaired each car with great skill, but even he could feel the chill in his heart. He would not have laughed, but he was not the sort of man to frown all the time. He did not know what else to do.

Everything in the repair factory seems to be covered with a layer of gray color, once had the joy, as if all of a sudden dissipated. Because of his love of maintenance, Hogan puts a lot of thought into the facility, working with his apprentices through the night to figure out how to fix cars. Even the purchase of an expensive special wrench to improve their repair skills made Hogan can make them laugh for a long time. But now all this, it seems to have become old memories, all become no fun. Apprentice boys who strive to create a relaxed atmosphere, want to let the teacher happy, Hogan also often can feel the atmosphere of joy, think in this atmosphere seems to be happy and smile, but he felt like looking into the sky and the water with some heavy grinds to the gap, or watching a silent comedy, want to be happy, don't happy, Want to laugh, but also hardly to smile, can only force the movement of the muscles on the face, make a smile expression.

The feeling of joy seemed to have left him.

Hogan's old friends invited him to the party, and for fear of spoiling the fun, Hogan didn't tell anyone about his ordeal. In a way, it may be that he does not want to repeat the helplessness of the pain in his mind. He smoked, drank, and talked with his friends as he would at any party, but it was not long before he was recognized as unusual. Hogan was forced to recount the ordeal and received a flood of reassurance.

In a way, Hogan has become a "smile depression."He did not want or dare to talk about his pain. He tried to go about his daily life, but it was hard to hide it. His weak smile was the obvious label of his pain."Afraid of being asked, tears in the throat pretend to be happy", perhaps only the mind is particularly sensitive and delicate, and talented people, in order to hide their inner suffering.

When your depressive symptoms set in, your mind sinks deep into a depressing, agonizing state of depression, and you try to repress the pain, perhaps the next step is to step into the dreaded abyss of bipolar disorder.

Hogan works with people who are physically and mentally healthy. When they learned of the tragedy in Hogan's family, they showed deep sympathy and helped him in every way they could. It had been a while, but everyone around Hogan noticed that something had changed in him. He was noticeably less reticent than he used to be, with fewer rambling jokes, and seemed moody all day. Even when explaining maintenance experience and knowledge, the tone of speech is no longer as cheerful and confident as in the past, and there is no interest in exploring new methods. He became more of a loner. There was still a smile on his face, but there was a sense of forlorn helplessness in it.

His colleagues are fully aware of how heartbreaking it is to lose a grandson they so eagerly anticipated, but they don't know what part of Hogan it has broken, and they don't know where to start to help him get back on his feet. The only hope is that Hogan himself will be strong enough to overcome the ordeal and start afresh.

Hogan's friends are healthy people, too. They learned the news at the party by accident, and they all felt sorry for Hogan. They fully understood Hogan's inner pain, even though years of friendship had enabled them to empathize with it, but they had trouble finding a way to ease his inner pain. If this happens to them, I'm afraid they have no way to speak of, can only rely on their inner strength to slowly resolve.

In fact, in this world, painful things happen almost all the time. Among Hogan's friends are people who have experienced this kind of loss, and who have bravely found themselves in the life that comes their way. They also kindly share their own journey with Hogan, but wonder if Hogan, who once immersed in the perfect life, will be brave enough to face his life again and again.

Feeling 5) Strong Remorse

Vera has just arrived in the city and found a new job. For Vera, everything here is brand new.

On the day of renting the house, Vera and the agent went to 10 locations in a row, three of which were repeated twice before they finally settled on the place Vera was satisfied with. Vera apologized repeatedly to the agent, thanked her, and then apologized again, feeling that she had been too much trouble and had delayed a lot of the agent's time. Fortunately, the matter was done, Vera specially slipped 200 yuan to the intermediary girl as a thank you and compensation.

Vera used to be a real estate agent in the same city. As a girl, she knew the hard work and the sadness in the process. At that time, she was also like the agent with all kinds of eccentric clients to look at the house, encountered strange things, sometimes even terrible danger. No one appreciated, apologized and tipped like her. This series of workplace encounters seems to have triggered something deep inside Vera, causing a huge change inside Vera. Though her disposition remained vivacity and cheerfulness, her heart, like stale bread, had added to it a great deal of cowardice and timidity. Unable to continue her work as a real estate agent, and unsure of how to heal the pain, she moved to another city, found a new job and started her life completely afresh.

Now that the house was settled, she wanted to

look for a job as soon as possible. She didn't want to be in a job that involved a lot of human contact, so she deliberately sought jobs that were more manual. However also indulge in the wage treatment and other issues, after several choices, she eventually became a well-known clothing brand saleswoman, in a bustling big shopping mall in the brand counter there to work. For Vera, the job of selling branded clothes is relatively less stressful than that of a real estate agent. And because of the sale of well-known brands of clothing, the customer experience is relatively simple. Vera is excited about her new job.

Next, she wanted to buy some things for her new home and get ready for her new career, so she went shopping at the supermarket. For Vera, who is new to the city, the supermarket is like a maze. She had no idea where she was looking for it, so she had to go back and forth between the shelves. When she passes someone, she whispers a word of apology, and if she gets in the way of a new customer, she nods a little and leaves, even if she hasn't yet chosen what she wants. She never stopped in the middle of the aisle, never stayed too long in the same spot, preferring to come back and browse a second time. In the Western world, such behavior is a very common common etiquette. But in contemporary China in the eastern world, this is a rare act, and some people stare at Vera with the audacity of a fool. Vera did not want to meet those eyes, even if it was offensive, and ignored him. This is a lesson Vera learned from her previous career.

At the checkout, Vera's shopping cart is about 30 centimeters away from the person in front of him, keeping it polite and easy for other guests to walk through. But the guests behind Vera unkindly put their shopping cart against her hips, and secretly pushed it, as if hoping that she would move forward and not leave a gap. Vera is helpless, apologizes softly, and slowly moves forward.

Vera spent a total of two hours shopping in the supermarket, and if you take a rough count of the number of apologies, it's almost a hundred. Although this kind of civility is common in the Western world, it is not practiced to this extent. Vera is like Junji Ito's "Apologize Devil" who apologizes like crazy. She always feels like she did something wrong, or something wrong, that has disturbed, affected, ruined their good mood, ruined their perfect day, or something like that. Those mildew like things, still ruthlessly attached in her heart.

Vera returns to her newly rented apartment and begins to clean up and furnish it. She walked slowly, so as not to disturb her neighbors downstairs. Everything was handled gently and carefully. Even if this is not a big room only oneself a person, but when farting also extra careful, afraid of startled to the surrounding neighbors. If no one had seen Vera live here, no one would have thought that this room was actually inhabited. The constant tension in Vera permeates everything she does. Even when she uses a computer keyboard to type, she caresses it as softly and slowly as if it were making loud noises. She didn't want to affect anyone. Once she accidentally knocked over a picture frame on her bedside table and apologized profusely to the air.

If you're familiar with the Chibi Maruko-chan

anime, the character Mr. Nakano would look like Vera if he were alive. Vera's behavior may have been more serious.

At work, Vera's politeness and enthusiasm endeared her to everyone. But the special attention shown by the male colleagues to Vera soon aroused the jealousy of the female colleagues. In this small brand, there are no romantic relationships between colleagues, not even flirtatious feelings. The jealousy is natural and pure.

The group leader told Vera that she should get familiar with the work as soon as possible. She should not only receive customers at the reception desk, but also help to carry goods and organize them in the warehouse. In this way, she could get familiar with all the procedures of the store in the shortest time, especially strengthen the grasp of the data of brand clothing type, size and so on. Vera doesn't know if all salespeople go through this process, but she embraces it and thinks it's a reasonable arrangement. But for Vera, the boxes are just too heavy. She managed to drag the trunk a few metres as hard as she could, and then had to rest for a while, feeling as if her legs were going to cramp.

It was only her first day on the job.

The group leader visits the warehouse and warns Vera about her questionable attitude towards her work. Vera apologizes and runs back to the box. When a male colleague came to help, Vera thanked him, apologized, thanked him, and apologized again. Male colleagues say you shouldn't be so polite. Vera apologized and expressed her gratitude.

Vera felt that she was really useless. She needed

help from other colleagues to sort out the goods, which not only delayed others' time, but also affected the interests of the company as a whole. If I weren't so useless, I wouldn't be in this situation. She thought she needed to compensate her colleagues for all the extra work they had put up with to help her. So she went to the food store and bought a lot of delicious snacks and drinks for her colleagues out of her own pocket, especially the one for the team leader. Fortunately, there are everything in the big shopping mall, but do not delay their own work time. Vera thanked, apologized, and shared out the treats. With that, Vera's uneasy feeling was calmed down.

Back home in the evening, Vera tiptoed her own meal, and as she ate, she began to reflect on the day's events.

Vera sometimes feels like she's overreaching, and civility doesn't have to be that way. In her heart of hearts, she also felt that she didn't need to apologize so wildly, that she didn't owe anyone anything, that she hadn't done anything wrong. Whenever think like this, the inner mood will instantly turn into grievances, sour nose, pain in the eyes, tears will drop down at a moment. Once immersed in this emotion, Vera's body becomes petrified, feeling guilty at every move she makes.

But as soon as she has to get on with life, or simply, she has to do the dishes and tidy up and go to sleep, her mind goes back to where it was before, and the rich, deep sense of self-blame floods through her once more.

Why is that?

If Vera goes back to her childhood, there may be

some answers. But apparently Vera isn't the kind of person to do that, and she didn't even think about this route. She doesn't even think it's a psychological problem. If a person is unable to fight against the malevolent outside world, or even is not allowed to fight against the intention, he will turn the mental spear of the intention to fight against himself, this is the origin of the sense of self-blame. Civilized manners are born of respect, and excessive self-discipline based on self-blame is essentially born of fear. These are two behaviors that appear to be the same in reality, but are completely different in nature.

How far do we have to go to get to this point?

The lady at the real estate agency who served Vera was a healthy person. She thinks Vera is a thoughtful, prudent, steady person who pursues perfection. Besides, she is kind and considerate and generous. She is a very good customer.

Vera's new colleagues are healthy people, too. They found Vera to be polite and warm, but often affected, as if trying to please everyone and acting calculating. The group leader felt as if Vera was deliberately showing weakness, and there was something strangely provocative about it. Female colleagues think that Vera is pretending to be weak and pure, pretending to be a pig and eating a tiger, while male colleagues generally like Vera's cheerful personality and polite and considerate performance.

In fact, Vera is really simple. She has neither ambition nor expectation. She really doesn't think of anything more than excessive worry about other people's attitude and endless remorse.

Feeling 6) Unable to Handle Stress

George is a very ordinary boy. He is a teacher in a university.

He teaches a course that has to do with ideological guidance, the kind of course that dresses up in moral guise and tells you how to tell right from wrong.

On the face of it, such a curriculum may seem normal, but basic human norms do require a degree of education and guidance. However, if you think carefully, you will find that, in fact, the universal human civilization etiquette norms, only need kindergarten level education can be all solved, do not need to set up special courses to educate us which things are absolutely right, which things are absolutely wrong. If we think a little bit more, we see the truth: Christians tell us that following God's will is the right thing to do, while pedophiles tell us that looking at children's genitals is the right thing to do.

Therefore, George is not supposed to think about this kind of course. In the course of "ideological guidance", both the teacher and the learner are forbidden to think and act. Unfortunately, thinking is one of George's great pleasures in life. And that fun contributed to his professional tragedy.

At the beginning of his professional life, George was full of ambition. He meticulously wrote down lesson plans, searched for materials, and enriched his classroom experience. He wants his classes to be unique, to be the kind of class that students can become addicted to no matter what kind of student is sitting in the classroom. To a certain extent, he has achieved this success. His lectures are not explanatory, but speech-style. At the end of each lecture, the classroom of more than 100 people will burst into warm applause in response to his efforts.

But this effort and success has had an unexpected side effect. In general, ideology-oriented courses are consistently considered the least useful for students if they do not have to get a grade for the course. However, because of George's efforts, the students' interest was aroused. Some students really began to think and pay attention to the course, and to think and study the theories and historical references in the textbook, which is a big taboo in the course.

The number of students asking questions in class is increasing, and the questions are getting closer and closer to the boundaries of real taboos. When George was in college, he majored in ideological theory. He was very well-behaved and did reasonably well in school, which means he didn't think much about what he was studying. Just memorize it, directly believe it, no need to think, more do not need to doubt.

But George's enthusiasm as a newcomer to the workplace puts him in a situation where he has to think. He couldn't answer the students' questions without doing some deep research and thinking. If he does not answer, his dream of creating a class that is uniquely good will die. This process, is about the so-called "teaching" it.

If it's a practical science subject like physics or chemistry, George isn't good at it, but he can fix it anyway. If it is impossible to explain, it can also be offered "something is up in the air, quantum mechanics; Einstein could not explain everything in the world, and Tesla also left countless residual thoughts, not to mention he was such a small unknown teacher.

But ideological guidance is a closed-loop course, where lies and taboos abound at the boundary with reality. It can explain everything in the universe as long as it doesn't touch the taboos, and as soon as the boundaries are touched, the whole system collapses. Like a child trying to cover up the consequences of misbehaving, he could come up with an infinite number of interesting and whimsical reasons. The world is not short of lies and reasons, and ideological guidance courses are one such reason. It could even become a system of its own, calling itself Maximalism.

Predictably, like George mind pure and kind young man, when he hit a real taboo border, heart is how vulnerable, how frightened, even if he on WeChat release information to express their shock and disbelief, then be banned WeChat and other social media titles, said he was incredible.

His inner reaction was like that of the great Newton, suddenly aware of the existence of "the first force of the universe," and anxious to find theological backing. Unfortunately, the ideology-guided course had already taught him that the world was materialistic, without a god.

Originally, he would happily walk into each classroom, to enthusiastically and actively face each lesson. Now he was terrified of the class, feeling like he was going to spread lies like crazy, to speak out naked in public. He didn't know what he was supposed to talk about in class, and he couldn't answer the "wacky" questions posed by the "very few" students. Should I continue my teaching duties, or should I spread the truth to these equally innocent children? He's really not sure. George even finds out what happened to him after he was reported by a student, which makes him even more terrified. If a teacher is reported by a student to be ideologically wrong, the teacher can not only be removed from the podium, but can even be sent to jail. These terrible thoughts tormented George's heart all the time, and finally made him unable to face his own class any more. He could not bear the heavy pressure from his heart.

It would take a few years for George to realize that the world was so obsessed with the "truth" that if you grasped it, you could bring truth and justice to the world. This mentality is no different than believing in maximalism and expecting a savior from the sky. The "truth" doesn't get us anywhere. It is also highly questionable whether there is such a thing as "truth" in the world. But as independent, free people, it is important that we judge and act by the goodness and courage that we have in our hearts. Isn't it a shame that we always expect others to stand up for justice, but we always give in to our own cowardice and meanness?

But then again, this is something that George is slowly learning from the twists and turns of his own life a few years later.

He could no longer face the classroom, and

when he looked at the people under the lectern, his legs trembled, he stammered, and his thoughts became incoherent. When preaching, there is no confidence, and eventually become a scripted reading robot. In order not to make mistakes, he added various propaganda videos released by the state's cultural propaganda department to his teaching plans to replace his own explanations. He seemed listless in class, ignored the students who raised their hands to ask questions, or simply went down in total depression.

The director of the Ideology Teaching and Research Section asked George to improve his classroom status. He asked him not to copy the lecture, let alone play so many videos, but to teach in a practical way. He also asked him to get off the platform and walk among the students, and teach in a very intimate manner.

George was horrified to realize that these were the practical applications of ideologically guided theories, using words to create a harmonious, happy, and happy atmosphere for people. The so-called "practical" lecture, is to only talk about those nice, good-looking, that is, those known as "positive energy" things. As for "bad reality", is there any truth? Did it really happen? Do you want to be reported and arrested and put in jail? George could only deal with it with a depressed attitude. He dared not say anything more, because if the director of the teaching and research section reported the report, the consequences would be more serious.

After the conversation, George still did what he wanted to do, because he couldn't find a way to reconcile himself, so he couldn't take the step to get off the stage.

The dean of the School of Ideology also came to talk to George. He hoped that George, a young man who had just entered the workplace, would give full play to his enthusiasm and energy and bring out all the energy of a young man so that he could have a good future. George was so overwhelmed by the encouragement that he couldn't see where his career was going. If he could not resolve the ideological conflict raging within him, his career would have been over.

To defuse the pressure of the dean's talk, George began to use the video time in class to learn Japanese, so that he could temporarily forget what he had just said.

In fact, there are many teachers of ideology-guided courses who do not take the content they are teaching seriously. Like many people who claim to be public servants, they can talk about clean and honest construction and correct life style during the day. In the evening, however, I can go back to one of my villas, count the hundreds of new property ownership certificates, and then spend the night with my No. N lover on a bed stuffed with money.

If you are not born into this class and do not have the ability to blend in, then all serious efforts are just asking for trouble.

George, as a man of integrity, as a man of sudden awakening, was under pressure. His rigid mind made him unable to take these theories he had studied seriously seriously, because he always thought that serious study is a virtue, "the university" is not to teach us: to know in the matter. In fact, the brain has been so rigid that awakening is simply a process of going to hell. The deeper the awakening, the deeper the hell.

He began to live like a zombie, but also slowly learned to muddle along. He didn't want to make any more effort, he didn't want to look forward to anything. He even added "lying flat" and "squatting at home" on the website, what appraisal title, paper, open class, all are to deal with. He could not explain the reality of the society to the students, and he knew that he could not change his future through efforts, so why bother himself and fatten up the leaders? It's nice to lie flat and feel free.

George couldn't take any more pressure. All the demands made on him and the work that involved him made his head ache and he felt sick. However, if he did not work, he could not earn money, and it would be difficult for him to make a living, so he had to bite the bullet.

He went to bed later and later. Even after an eight-hour day and gritting his teeth to prepare for the next day's classes, he would stay up late. He doesn't do anything with a clear meaning or purpose. He just curls up under the covers with his phone, reading boring news and posts, and doesn't want to fall asleep. There's a psychological term called "Revenge Bedtime Procrastination," and George apparently already has it.

After going to bed late, the next day was even worse. George seemed to have aged several years in a short period of time, to the sighs of everyone around him.

Teacher George's students are all healthy people. They found him to be a vibrant and enthusiastic teacher, a far from the ideological class teachers of the past. They liked George's passion in class, liked to listen to his quotations, and admired the depth of his theoretical knowledge. But even before the end of a semester, he had undergone a strange change, as if he had lost his soul, and went to class every day in a trance. The students felt that the troublemakers had seriously affected the teacher's mood by asking questions, and out of sympathy they stopped asking questions. But George never recovered and became even more depressed.

George's leaders and colleagues are also healthy people. When they interviewed George, they were very fond of this passionate and energetic young man. In particular, George's solid theoretical foundation fully demonstrated his careful study attitude and diligent and rigorous academic temperament. This is a very valuable quality in a young population, and it makes everyone think highly of George's growth potential. I don't know what happened, but within a very short time George was depressed and depressed. Well-meaning colleagues all speculated that he might have been broken up in love, or that something had happened to his family. Although they asked around in vain, George seemed to be pretending to be mysterious. The leaders and colleagues have tried their best to help George, but the effect is not good. Everyone feels very sorry and hopes that George can get out of his psychological haze as soon as possible.

In fact, life is not an academic, there is no need to take it so seriously. Sometimes the stress we hurl at ourselves is caused by our inability to resolve a problem in our heart. Try asking yourself, are you trying to be perfect? Did you suddenly discover some truth about life? Can't let go of some kind of moral law? If you think about it, there is always a reason for being depressed.

Feeling 7) Intense Anxiety: Delusion of Persecution

For whatever reason, Sally seems to be having mixed feelings these days.

Sally is an ordinary worker in a food processing factory. The factory produced all kinds of pickled food, and she was responsible for adding flavoring to the washed food according to the recipes. It wasn't a big factory, but it wasn't a mom-and-family business, and when it came to adding flavoring, two other workers did the same job.

In the field of food production, competition is not particularly fierce, no matter what kind of food is produced, as long as the advertisement is in place, the brand name sounds good, basically there will be a good market. But even so, as a worker in a food processing factory, wages are still low. And because competition for positions is so intense, assembly line workers who make mistakes, don't work overtime, whine, or just get annoyed by the foreman are quickly laid off and replaced by new people. There is no special skill required to work on the assembly line, which makes the workers really like screws, screwed on and off at any time, with few people caring what they think, let alone providing institutional or legal safeguards for their labor.

Sally didn't feel that she had any advantages over others that would make her a permanent worker. Besides, she didn't want to spend her whole life in a factory like this. But the reality is that without a job, life can quickly become difficult. Sally felt that she needed to find some quick and easy ways to make money as soon as possible in order to achieve her financial freedom.

Under the recommendation of her friend, Sally began to invest in stocks. This is the beginning of Sally's increasingly complicated feelings.

The stock market is changing rapidly. Sally's friend, out of kindness, introduced the way of investing in the stock market to Sally because she got some benefits from it. But neither Sally nor her friends fully realized the risks involved in stock investment. They just rushed into the field with the good fantasy of making a quick profit and a small amount of savings.

Although this investment is not much, it has accounted for 90% of Sally's total personal savings, because her friend told her that the more investment, the greater the return, and proved this point for Sally intuitively with her own stock investment experience. This aroused Sally's imagination and expectations, so she naturally put a large amount of savings on the line.

To the investors, the little money she had in the

stock market was as good as no money at all. But to Sally, it was a big deal. She didn't discuss it with her parents in advance. She thought she was an adult and could make her own decisions. There's really nothing wrong with that idea. But the problem is that there are rules to everything Sally thinks she can decide. It's not really up to Sally.

In short, within three days of joining the stock market, Sally had her entire fortune tied up.

Looking at the green chart on the screen, Sally knew that she had lost most of the savings she had worked for many years, although she was not fully familiar with the meaning of the data symbols. All at once she felt a great tension rush through her body, and with it a great uneasiness, a feeling of heaviness in her head, a queasiness in her stomach, and a slight shiver all over her.

Luckily, Sally's job wasn't done standing on a single-plank bridge, for if she had, she would have fallen instantly.

The assembly line never waiting for anyone, and before Sally could fully feel what was happening inside her, her colleagues had already handed her bags of salt, sugar and a whole bunch of other ingredients. She quickly took over and added according to the recipe. The orderly array of food cans in front of her, like black Wells, made Sally's truncated sense of vertigo come up again, and a strong sense of uneasiness invaded her mind again.

As you can imagine, in this mood, Sally's ability to correctly identify the seasonings in her hand is really questionable.

Sally could not control her anxiety and fear. Her

mind was full of the floating green charts. She did not know what she was doing. The food had an unusual dark red tint. But in a factory like this, does anyone care about color?

Spurred on by the investment, Sally's uneasiness spread like mold during the rainy season. She almost wants to keep her eyes on the ever-changing K-chart, expecting to see dramatic reversals in her stocks. Unfortunately, nothing happened, and she wasn't able to pay close attention. After the investment failed, the pickle factory's work became extremely important.

Sally sprinkles salt and worries about whether her stock price will continue to fall, sugar and worries about whether she will lose all her money, pepper powder and whether she will need to borrow money to pay the rent, cumin powder and whether her parents will pass out if they find out.

When a kind of anxiety that we have never experienced suddenly takes possession of us, it will multiply wildly to any possible place, as if to put on a strange pair of dark glasses for your brain, whatever you look at, whatever you think, is black.

Sally was in such a bad state. She thought of her friends' deceit from her investment failures, of her savings that disappeared completely, of borrowing money, of her parents' grief, of her job loss, of her desperation, of her street life, of her suicide by hanging herself. If you've ever experienced anxiety, you know how this series of hallucinations can happen.

After work, Sally decided to confront her friend first. Two people were chatting at a diner when Sally saw that all of her friend's stocks were going green. It wasn't a good thing, but at least she felt a little better because her friend wasn't cheating her. The friend is very want to open, she said this is normal phenomenon, the stock, ups and downs is normal, such as the whole line wave red time, don't make yourself happy crazy on the line. When I was leaving, my friend suddenly asked Sally, "Have you changed the recipe? The recent pickles taste strange. This question scared Sally out of her mind, but she didn't dare to show it to her face. She had to fudge her friend that she had changed the formula recently, and seemed to be making some kind of reform.

Sally knew that it was her own mistake, but she dared not tell her friend the truth, because she was not even sure whether the pickles sold in the market were safe or not. Salt, sugar and paprika are not the only ingredients in the recipe. There are also many food-grade chemical additives. Although it is food grade, it has strict requirements on the amount. If it is added more, the consequences will be very terrible.

If you were Sally and thought of this in a split second, would you have the guts to tell your friends the truth?

Sally was afraid to say. She did not even dare to tell her friend to his face that she would not eat the pickles for the time being. Because once she gave those warnings, there was no hiding the truth.

But clearly, this is much more frightening than a stock drop. The anxiety, the fear, the horror, the uneasiness in Sally's heart all came back again, and they all came back more fiercely.

Will there be a food poisoning incident? Sally's

mind went crazy over the matter. The most important thing is that she is not sure whether she put more additives or less additives, those days of state, it is like sleepwalking. Her mind was so full of anxiety that she could not judge anything, and her memory was not very coherent.

Now it's getting worse. She doesn't even know when she returned to her rented room.

If someone's life was endangered by eating these pickles, they would be traced back to the factory and arrested by the police, wouldn't they? Mom and Dad will go crazy if they find me be arrested to jail, right? I heard that prison is very scary, I must be severely beaten, right?

Just as Sally was dreaming, her phone vibrated. It was a text message. Shaking, Sally clicked the message. It was from the team leader of her own production line at the pickle factory. It said: Come to my office tomorrow.

It's over. I've been found out. I'm going to jail tomorrow. Sally looked at the message and couldn't stop her tears.

Or die."Sally thought wildly. For some reason, a picture of herself hanging from the beam of her rented house flashed into her mind, her tongue hanging out and her eyes whitened in incredible detail, and she shuddered and nearly ran out of the house.

She lit all the lights in the house, drew the curtains tightly, and tucked herself in. The warmth and light soothed her anxiety. She turned on the video playing APP on her mobile phone, and there appeared a variety show that she loved very much.

Artists on the screen shuttled back and forth, which was very lively. The noisy voices temporarily paralyzed her fear in her heart.

What on earth will happen tomorrow? The group leader must have sold me out. He passed me several times while I was at work looking at the stocks. He must have made a mental note of it, though he didn't say anything at the time. The police must have been waiting for me there, and I must have lost my life if this pickle had killed anyone. What am I going to do? Although the variety show was as lively and interesting as usual, Sally couldn't help thinking about these terrible things. She didn't even know the tears were dripping onto the quilt.

The next day, as the sun shone, her anxiety seemed to ease, but the illusion of terror still occupied her mind. She braved her way to the factory and shuffled into the team leader's office.

The group leader said, "Sally, you seem to have something on your mind recently. Are you in love? But work needs to work seriously, can not always look at the phone, delayed production, how can we make money? Also, this is the new recipe. From today on, follow this recipe.""And she handed a piece of paper to Sally.

That's all the group leader said.

The mad anxiety in Sally's heart seemed to dissipate in a moment. The stock goes up and down, let it go as it pleases. Sally decided to get things done when she got to work. The fact that pickles contain chemical additives that can cause death is so terrible that Sally does not want to go through the horror anxiety again.

Sally's friend is a healthy person. She knows that Sally is also the kind of person who is cheerful and they have always hit it off well. But she had no idea that the loss in the stock market would have a significant impact on Sally's mood, turning her from a chatty girl into a taciturn, suspicious girl who suspected that she was setting her up. Fortunately, his stock is also falling, clearing the wrong. But when he thought about it, his friend wondered if he was crazy. His stock was falling, but he felt lucky. Calculate, sentient beings drink enough water, friends are still good, money is not so important.

Sally's group leader on the production line is also an awareness of physical and mental health. He always thinks that Sally is a good worker with warm, cheerful personality, active and serious work, which is a very important thing for a food processing enterprise. Despite all the personnel quality of the food processing industry is the good and bad are intermingled, and practical, low wages, heavy physical strength, hard work environment, it is difficult to recruit excellent employees and even the general staff are not easy to recruit, it is conceivable that the tepid small food processing enterprises in what will be carried. Fortunately, the human gut is basically strong, so the fault tolerance rate in the food processing industry is even much looser than the mechanical processing field. Of course, this does not mean that production workers can do whatever they want.The group leader was very worried about Sally's distraught state these days, but he didn't know exactly what had happened. After several observations, he thinks it may have something to do with love. During her recent work, Sally always secretly looked at her mobile phone. After reading it, she began to feel listless and her work seemed like sleepwalking. Hoping to alert Sally to a new flavor of pickles being made at the factory, he texted her to come to the office for a chat. In a small business like this, going to the team leader's office is a very serious business. After the interview, the group leader did see the change in Sally's mental outlook, so he was more sure of his judgment. Sally really seemed to be in love.

Feeling 8) Weakness of the Soul:

Loneliness and Isolation

Evan was alone in the room. Although it was daylight and the sun was shining outside, his room was dark with the curtains closed.

He is playing a computer game, the role of the game flash show move, quick, decisive, very powerful, rushed up the enemy are all killed.

Evan has been living this life for a long time. He lives alone in this room, eats, drinks and scatters are all solved in the room, unless in a coma, he will not take the initiative to leave the room.

This room was his bedroom, and he lived with his parents, who had no access to his room except to bring him food through a crack under the door.

Evan had seen a film called " Who R U" the

horror film, which describes a hiding in his room playing games, five years without leaving the house the little boy, his mother have been through the note and boy, until finally the truth revealed, you just know that in fact the boy would have been turned into a mummy. Was it a complaint, or was the boy's mother's evil spirit? It doesn't matter. What matters is that Evan has lived his own life.

He felt that one day, he would become a mummy like that. If it turned into a spirit of resentment, he vowed to wreak havoc on the world. But if you can't become a ghost, it is not a bad thing, they must have been completely liberated from this mortal world.

But it was only when Evan was just starting his life. Within six months even this thought had completely vanished from his mind. He had no desire, no desire, no love, no hate. In his sensory world, the passage of time becomes very blurred, and the feelings of life and death are no longer so obvious. At times he even wondered if he might be dead, in the process of becoming a mummy. To confirm this process, Evan could stare into a mirror and remain motionless for two days.

Looking at this, you can say that these descriptions are overblown. But are you really sure you won't fall into that mood one day?

Evan wasn't born this way.

Dating back to 10 years ago, when he was in adolescence, he was full of curiosity about the world just like his friends. Their curiosity not only made them pay attention to the changes in the outside world, but also aroused great interest in their own changes under the impact of hormones. Young men and girls in this period are like the sea anemones living in the deep sea, stretching out countless tentacles around, to sense and explore this magical world. These tentacles are sensitive and delicate, with their own immature personality, to understand everything around them, and to use the feedback of everything around them to continue to shape their own soul.

In a society that was relatively closed to civilization and culture, these kids circulated adult-world books like *Lady Chatterley's Lover*. I do not know from whom it began, but there were always such books circulating in their hands, and when one read them, they were immediately passed on to the next, and a third person would come and take orders. When the book Lady Chatterley's Lover reached Evan, Andy ordered it from him.

The work produced by Sir David Herbert Lawrence in his "Primal Pilgrimage" project is clearly more sincere and appealing than the backwater and hypocrisy of moral instruction in moral lessons. Moreover, for human society, knowledge derived from sincerity is obviously more nourishing than all false claims, which is particularly important in both natural and social sciences. If children, with their natural simplicity, are generally averse to certain subjects, perhaps grown-ups should look at every process of their education and see if there is something insincere behind it.

If we had a more sincere and scientific approach to human reproduction, Mr. Lawrence's work might not have caused so much controversy in so many countries around the world.

But we all know that the more forbidden something is, the more it will have a special attraction to human beings. This is especially true for teenagers. Andy thought Evan would finish the book quickly and get his turn. But Evan forgot the appointment and lent the book to someone. Although he apologized to Andy and took the book back to Andy as soon as possible, the process was still like a sharp thorn in Andy's heart, which made him unforgettable.

Andy quickly finished reading *Lady Chatterley's Lover* and returned the book to Evan's house as promised. Evan wasn't home. His father is at home. Andy hesitated. Without hesitation, he handed the unencased book to Evan's father, telling him that it was Evan's book and that he must give it to Evan. Oh, and there are several realistic illustrations in that book, which is one of the main reasons why this great work of art and literature is so popular among restless teenagers.

Evan, who has a passion for painting, was taking a training course in painting. When he returned home, his mind was caught off guard, and he was cursed and beaten by his father. In the process of beating and scolding, he learned the cause of the matter, the mood becomes very complicated. Later, his mother came home from work and, after a brief review of what had happened, joined in.

In China, there is a popular saying that "beating is love, scolding is love", which is specially used to educate children. In 1987, there was even a famous six-episode children's TV series, Good Dad Bad Dad (directed by Yin Li), in which a famous children's song called I Have a Good Father, with lyrics like: I have a good father...Which father does not call names, which children do not get beaten, beat is to kiss to scold is love, or that good father!(quoted from Sina: https://k.sina.cn/article_6403017762_17da64c22001 00ij8n.html)

The children's TV series was released in China and won the first prize and the outstanding scriptwriting award of the Ninth National Excellent TV Series Flying Appreciation Award for Children's TV Series. It has been praised online by people born in the 1970s and 1980s as one of the "ten most memorable TV series". This is a Stockholm syndrome home.

Of course, this kind of education is not accessible to everyone, like Evan. But there are many who believe in it, like Evan's parents. What happens if they happen to get together? Young Evan couldn't fight his parents, and his soul wasn't strong enough to recognize his situation and form a form of resistance, so he had to channel his hatred into his own heart, into his own cowardice.

Don't just think it's an accident, it's the norm. Those who believe in violence education will carry out violence education at any time, for any reason, anytime and anywhere. The most common is when children question their authority. Right or not, is not important, obedience, is the key. This kind of behavior is completely consistent with the autocratic pattern that the country has been dominating society for thousands of years.

In this incident, Evan is once again subjected to horrific domestic violence, as well as feeling betrayed by his friends, and has serious doubts about the trust between people. He felt that he really had to take responsibility for what had happened, and could even say that he was the cause of it. But are the consequences too great? There was no kindness or compassion in the messages that came back to him. Are humans such selfish and hypocritical creatures? If what was written in that book was not supposed to happen, then where did I come from?

It is a backward and ignorant society, but it is better than a completely brutalized society or a completely deceitful society. This is not to say that there are no psychological problems in a more civilized and advanced society, but that such a state of society is more likely to cause problems for people's souls. People seem to live in the "fog", do not know when will die from the monster's mouth.

Evan's mood became very dull. Outside, he and his friends continued to communicate seemingly normally, but the mood was so low that it was almost as if he were performing The Sorrows of Young Werther himself. At home, he stayed in his room as much as possible. He avoided all sounds and all possible communication.

Evan's parents are worse than shit to the outside world, but they're like king and queen at home. They not only like domestic violence education, but also adhere to the concept of "the bite is worse than the heart". In contemporary Chinese street culture, this is also considered a very good word to whitewash any kind of verbal violence among the people. It means: its mouth is like a knife, and its words are dirty and filthy, as if the blade could cut into your soul, but its heart is soft as tofu, full of kindness and love.

Do you believe?

Beat your pet. Swearing at your pet. See how they react.

So even though Evan has retreated to his bedroom, his parents are still proud of their stinky educational views, their silly outlook on life, and their blabbermouth in all sorts of situations. Evan can't accept it, but he can't fight it. He represses his feelings and anger in a cold, crazy way at home, and tries his best to be transparent.

However, Evan's behavior escalates his parents' violent behavior. In the spare time, everything Evan does, every movement, every thought, even every look and expression, will be judged and judged by his parents. For Evan, every second he faces his parents in life is a soul-crushing experience.

His soul grew weaker and smaller, and almost completely lost the courage and strength to face the world.

In this way, he endured for a number of years, and finally was no longer that weak boy. But his state of mind had been ruined by years of mental depression. The painting he loved, which once depicted the most dazzling works in the class, has now become the most common imitation level of art school students because of the lack of individuality. He can't create, he can't brainstorm. There was little encouragement or praise in his life. Instead, his life was filled with vicious taunts and curses from his parents. He didn't know which of his actions was right or good, and he wasn't sure which would be motivated by kindness, so he almost completely lost his individuality and creativity. The tentacles of his soul stretched about him could not bring back nourishment for his growth, and his soul shriveled.

He has also sent out resumes to various companies and received job offers in painting and design. But in interpersonal communication, his words and deeds are gentle and polite, but lack of confidence. Treat your manager respectfully, but can't stand the pressure of routine work. Be overly cautious and never initiate communication. The completed work can only be considered as the technology in place, but it is difficult to achieve the visual impact requirements of graphic design work, always angular, always plain as water, not enough dynamism. As a graphic designer, this is a very fatal flaw. Soon after, he was fired by the company.

When they come home, the parents are always complaining, sarcastic, mocking, sarcastic, and cursing. Evan's parents threatened him with no financial support and no food, saying he was a trash man whose destiny was to pick up trash. Evan has endured it all in silence, for years anyway.

After several failed jobs, he stopped looking for work and planned to do something on his own. As a common class, self-employment is full of hardships, and it requires full enthusiasm and strong spiritual strength to find a path suitable for oneself. Evan's mental strength is very weak. He often feels lonely and helpless, with no one to sit beside him and listen attentively and quietly to his inner voice.

I'm used to it anyway. This was the most common consolation he could say to himself.

Evan knows the despair when his parents curse

him a lot. He felt as if his family had been cursed, as in the story of 112 Ocean Drive. He also wanted to try the revenge story of Jennifer Pan, a Toronto girl he had found on the Internet. But the weakness of his soul made him lazy to do these things. He didn't dare, and he didn't want to.

If you're in the mood to check out the world's most famous serial killers, horrific murderers, evil murderers, and juvenile delinquents, big and small, you'll often find one horrible family after another. These scum parents create these murderers with stupidity and violence and then let them become a disaster. The law of the world is so unsound, and human civilization is so low ignorance, can indulge such men and women to give birth to children, and they do not have to create out of the murder of the devil to bear half a dime of punishment. Domestic violence by parents against their children is tantamount to violence against the entire human world, and such bastards can get away with it with impunity, even earning the praise of "Tiger Mom Wolf Dad". In the human world, there are still countries to recognize and indulge this kind of behavior, and this kind of country, can also pretend to be an ancient Oriental civilization, it is shameless and ridiculous.

In fact, if you think about it carefully, aren't those parents who engage in domestic violence the evil products of the authoritarian, violence-obsessed, long-term ignorance of the law as a plaything of the government? And here on Earth, there are many countries that have largely eliminated this evil product. In more civilized countries, the child is regarded as God's angel to earth, not only as a continuation of the life of his parents, but also as an independent individual who is treated with equal respect, regardless of age. In countries with sound laws, when domestic violence occurs, the perpetrator is severely punished and receives a legal ban on contacting the victim or approaching the victim's living area. The two elements of "high civilisation" and "sound law" go hand in hand, the antidote to dictatorship and violence. The social basis of these two elements is the love and kindness of adults as parents towards children. Without this kind of love, it is difficult for children to grow up to be civilized people, and the lack of civilized people, also will never be born with civilized society, institutions and institutions are only the outer garment of human civilization.

Children need education, also need guidance, but do not need to beat, do not need violence. If you don't know the difference, take a word of advice from me: Don't have children. Don't ruin the world. When you've learned the lessons of child-rearing and figured out the lessons of parenthood, it's not too late to have another child.

I also advise you not to associate with parents who deliberately, persistently, enjoy child abuse. No matter how they decorate themselves as elegant, gorgeous, noble, ordinary, good, helpless, they are not human at heart. Unfortunately, they are still people under human law, so we can't swat them like flies and mosquitoes. For those of you who have not experienced domestic violence, I am 100% sure you cannot understand what this means. But people who have experienced domestic violence, especially people who have experienced severe domestic violence, I think you will recognize this argument.

Evan didn't do anything out of line. He had a good heart and didn't want to hurt anyone. He just lived in his little bedroom day after day. He decided to close all communication channels with the outside world, no longer for their own life to do any effort. In his eyes, his lonely self, all actions are futile. His soul was too weak to be Dr Faustus.

Evan's friends are all healthy people. In their eyes, Evan is just like any other teenager. He loves to laugh and play, and he is a good gamer. When we are looking for the secret book of customs clearance, he has taken the lead in completing the difficulty of "zero person cut" which belongs to the pure challenge of self. He was very handsome, gentle and shy, and always had a soft laugh in his voice. He was great company. Andy, one of his friends, was full of apologies for his behavior of returning the book. He did not know how his behavior had affected Evan, but he vaguely sensed that the influence might be very bad. He apologized a thousand times in his mind, but he never had the courage to tell Evan to his face.Whether Evan remembers the incident or not, Andy's feelings of regret endure to this day.

Evan has worked for companies where managers and employees were all physically and mentally healthy. They thought Evan did OK in the interview, but he's been in a bad mood ever since he started. His painting skills are good, it can be seen that after a long period of training, but for the "seek new and different hot" graphic design market, steady and steadfast is not a good quality, lack of confidence is even worse. As a designer, painting skills can be further cultivated, but mentality and creativity are not easy to obtain. Although Evan has a good character, due to the size of the company, he is unable to pay for his personality, so he has no choice but to resign.

Feeling 9) Endless Suicidal Delusions

Standing by the railing on the roof, Jason wanted to jump. But every time he moved under the urge of this desire, his mind kept on showing the sad pictures of those who had thrown themselves from buildings. This is the 15th floor of the building. If you jump from here, you'll burst your brains out. He had searched the Internet for information about people who had committed suicide by jumping from buildings. He had seen pictures of people who had died, and he was terrified.

Thanks to those who died, he stopped Jason from committing suicide by jumping from a building at the cost of his life.

When you think about it, humans are a really strange species, and suicide is one of the strangest behaviors of this species. When there is a news report about a suicide, Jason will pay special attention to the identity of the person who committed suicide and try to guess what might have made them choose to kill themselves. In his understanding, it seems that only people who have a hard life and survive at the bottom of society choose to commit suicide. But after reading so much news, he found that this wasn't the case. Instead, it was those who were successful and successful that seemed to be more likely to follow that path.

Perhaps suicides among the underclass are rarely reported by the news media, neither newsworthy, nor socially meaningful, nor even entertaining. If there are some suicide cases that can cause social uproar, even if the media does not report them, the whole society will hear about them and make a great fuss about them.

A few years ago, Jason accidentally became the first person to find the body of a man who had hanged himself while walking during his lunch break. As an unsociable man, he would go out for a walk along the river path after his dinner in the company cafeteria. It is desolate and remote, overgrown with bushes and many newly planted saplings, and is of little interest to those who are used to office work. Jason loves it here.

One day, as he was taking his usual walk, he came near a young tree that had just been planted when he noticed a figure hiding behind it. He was nervous, thinking he had met a robber, just waiting for the figure to jump out and shout "rob", he was ready to turn around and run. But for a few seconds as he stared, the figure behind the tree did not move. Was it waiting for him to approach?

The shadow behind the tree swayed with the cold wind, as it passed suddenly. There was a smell of earth and vegetation, which seemed to be mixed with something not so often smelled of "dead bodies". It's salty and slightly smelly, a far cry from the overpowering stench of carrion, and even if you've never smelled it before, you can tell it when you smell it. Jason finally realized what he had encountered. He was a little confused, but then he remembered to call the police.

Until the police car and ambulance arrived, he stood quietly in front of the body, looking at it carefully with a sense of confusion. He was a rural man in his 40s, identified by his dusty striped T-shirt and worn jacket at the bottom. Not even the scruffiest urban white-collar would ever dress like this. His shoes were half-new sneakers and covered with dust. The side pocket of his trousers was turned out, perhaps from the rope, for the dead man did not notice it and did not put it back. Because of the stasis of the blood, the dead man's face was dark brown, rather than the usual livid hue of the dead. His knack for tying ropes was so good that when his head slipped into the noose, it easily pulled tight as his weight sank, keeping most of his blood in his veins on his head and leaving a fine line of veins in the middle and upper part of his neck.

Perhaps hanging is a more painful form of suicide, the victim's face with a relaxed expression of pain, eyes slightly open, only the edge of his black eyes on the lower edge of the upper eyelid exposed. The nose is slightly wrinkled and seems to be suffering from a very itchy feeling. The lips were slightly open, but no tongue was sticking out. If a person who has died from hanging is not treated as quickly as possible, the tongue will be ejected and grow longer with time as the rotting gas in the body increases and the pressure in the body cavity builds up. It is the same principle that corrupts the giant, that a fetus is born after death, and that the corpse suddenly twists, farts, croaks, or even explodes. Fortunately, the body was found by Jason in time and didn't go that far.

The victim, who was about 170cm tall, had hanged himself from a newly planted tree with a twine commonly used in rural areas. His feet are less than 20cm from the ground and his head is less than 30cm from the branch hanging from the rope, which is only 10cm thick and thin. These small numbers, all in the deceased show the great determination to commit s uicide. Jason thought of the news that on May 15, 2014, a man named Shen hanged himself with his feet on the ground in Chuangxiangxiang, Qinhuai District, Nanjing. He also thought of those forensic records of him hanging from the doorknob or lying flat on his bed with a brick hanging. He compared these methods in his mind.

Jason didn't leave until the police arrived and finished recording his statement. He took a close-up of the dead man but didn't tell anyone. He followed the various news outlets over the next few days and saw nothing about it.

Why always can think of suicide? This is a big mystery that has been weighing on Jason for a long time. The reasons for suicidal feelings must be different for each person. Simple analysis, the sudden great disappointment to the social reality, or the sudden great despair to the status quo of self-survival, may be an important factor to promote the suicidal thoughts of ordinary people.

Jason is a very rational person. He not only suffers from such constant suicidal thoughts, but also is curious about the root of such thoughts.

The suicidal thought born suddenly, although the impact is terrible, but it is relatively easy to resolve, after persuasion and emotional counseling, often can be stopped, and then go back to the ordinary people, for grain laments, living in old age, sickness and death grief.

But Jason's mental state is unusual and difficult to resolve. His life has not come to an end at all, and there is no death-threatening dilemma happening, and even the material life is relatively good, but he is still unable to get rid of the terrible obsession with death.

For some reason, he had been depressed for a long time in his life. He could not feel joy. He thought that anyone who was happy and laughing was stupid, but in order to pretend to fit in, he had to pretend to be happy. Everything in life seems to him dull and dull and rigid, but if you ask him what kind of life would make him happy, he can only answer "no". As long as he is living, there is no life to make him happy. So, there's no way but die to him.

When a person is depressed and has progressed to this point of wanting to die, it's a very scary state of mind.

Jason often thinks that perhaps a pen piercing the throat is a good way to die. He had several pens that he loved very much, and when he was working he would lay them out on the table in a row. Pens come in different sizes and colors, so they can be used in a variety of ways. Jason imagined himself being stabbed through the throat with a pen. When he woke up, he would occasionally shake his whole body.

He also imagines himself jumping out of the window of his own floor, which is the third floor, and it doesn't seem like a terrible death. Due to his career, Jason once had the opportunity to get close to the body of someone who committed suicide by jumping from a building. It was a pair of girls who jumped hand in hand from the height of 20 floors. Their limbs were twisted and their brains were splashed in all directions, which gave Jason a strong shock to his soul. Though his knowledge of death was not inconsiderable, the enormity of it was daunting. In a low voice and reverent voice, he used a Buddhist mantra to transcend the couple, praying that they could continue to get together in the afterlife and achieve the happiness they were looking forward to. Because of this experience, whenever Jason wanted to jump off a building, his fear would arise spontaneously.

He imagines being electrocuted by wire, taking detergent, drinking too much alcohol or taking too many drugs, being hit by a car, hit in the head by a wheel, drowning in a company fish tank, tumbling down stairs, and so on. When he gets home and is alone, he imagines shooting himself, hanging himself from the beam, turning on the gas, pouring gasoline on it and burning it. But he never thought of slitting his wrists, stabbing himself to death, drowning in a bathtub, or using grenades.

There were times when he wanted to hurt his colleagues, or kill them, in the same way he had killed himself.

At other times, he even felt as though someone was calling his name, telling him in a hollow, half-true voice to die and to describe to himself the beauty of death. It happened so often that for a while he believed he must be possessed by some evil spirit. The voice was ethereal, improbable, indistinguishable from gender, and, crucially, indistinguishable from reality. At work, this evil call is relatively rare, but when he is alone at home, when he sinks into a deep depression, the annoying voice often comes out of nowhere.

Jason even felt that his house was cursed with death, and he was enveloped in a dark mist of gloom. Every day brings bad luck, bad problems, and failure at everything you do. Jason believes in the Buddha, but he feels as if he is the one who has been abandoned by the Buddha.

Fortunately, when he hit rock bottom, he would try to save himself from the brink of suicide. This is a very difficult job, but it is not impossible. He would go out and bask in the sun when he most wanted to die, and if there was no sun, he would start listening to music. He would grab a pen and instantly write down what he was feeling, each word like a rope to rescue himself.

This suicidal obsession is like a contaminated ocean wave, coming in and then rolling away. Every time he struggled through this terrible emotion, Jason would think carefully about the process he had gone through. What on earth triggered his strong desire to commit suicide? There is no strong work pressure, no terrible economic dilemma, no terrible life contradictions, and no apocalyptic survival dilemma. Life is so ordinary, plain, sunny, blue sky and white clouds. Jason can hardly imagine why he was in the state of wanting to die before. The only plausible explanation is probably the "curse of the undead".

When you look at what you write in that mindset, there are a lot of crazy thoughts, and a lot of paranoid thoughts. It seems that this paranoid, manic psychological state, prompted the depression of their own into the desperate situation of death. If you can suddenly recognize this situation in the depression, it should be able to save yourself. It seems that when writing these words, it is probably this sudden understanding of the "paranoid" and "manic" demons in the process, he accidentally cracked their evil curse, for his own left a chance of survival.

Jason kept all the crazy words on the paper and burned them all.

Jason works with people who are physically and mentally healthy. They have a good impression of Jason. They think he is modest, polite, measured and low-key. He is a modest gentleman. Colleagues also highly recognize Jason's working ability. He can handle multiple tasks at the same time, arrange his time reasonably and complete the project efficiently, which is something not everyone can do. Although they all know that Jason doesn't fit in, it's nothing. People have different personalities, isn't it normal? Work is already boring, and each individual geek is the best spice in the workplace.

Feeling 10) Horrifying Visions of the End

It's 3a.m. in the morning.

In the home.

Mark slept restlessly, with all sorts of strange dreams swirling in his mind. If you look closely, you can see Mark's eyes moving rapidly under his flared LIDS, sometimes turning completely white, sometimes looking straight at someone.

This state is the rapid eye movement (REM) phase of sleep in humans, sometimes occurring as many as three to four times out of every eight hours of sleep. Each time it happens, it may last a few minutes, or it may last a long time. During this time, dreams flood, perhaps dozens of dreams pass in quick succession, but people usually remember only one or two.

Mark dreamed of his home. He was standing in the dark kitchen. Outside the window, the moon was bright, but it could only reach the ledge. Mark looked around as if he were a stranger, feeling that the place was familiar, but had a strange smell to it.

In the kitchen, near the aisle, there is a huge refrigerator, a pure white box that appears ice in the dark. Mark leaned against the fridge door and peered out to the end of the aisle. There was their bedroom. Jasmine, his wife, was sleeping in bed with Mark by her side.

It was dark, and Mark, leaning on the refrigerator door, couldn't see into the bedroom. Mark wanted to ask his wife to help him, so he called softly   toward   the   bedroom, "Jasmine...Jasmine...Jasmine...Jasmine......"

His wife didn't respond, but he thought he heard his own voice. He looked up from the bed. He heard his own voice and saw himself looking out of the fridge into the bedroom.

Mark, leaning over the refrigerator door, saw his head look up, but he continued to whisper to Jasmine. As he lay in bed, Mark suddenly felt very frightened and let out a repressed scream. It was a scream, but it was hoarse and scratchy, and the tone was completely distorted. This heightened Mark's fear, so much so that he woke up screaming.

His wife, Jasmine, had also woken up, earlier than Mark. In the moonlight, she saw Mark struggling uneasily in his sleep. Then she opened her eyes.

Jasmine asked softly, "Have you had a bad dream?"

Mark said, "Yes. Did you hear me shouting?"

Jasmine said, "I didn't hear you. But you were just saying 'killed' in a trembling voice, several times."

Mark looked back, but he had no memory of the dream. He didn't know what he had seen in the dream.

Obviously, Jasmine felt frightened, but she was also very curious, so she continued, "What did you dream about in your dream? When you said, 'I've killed someone,' you were terrified. Your voice was shaking. It was like you had seen a ghost, not killed someone."

Mark had to say, "I don't know. I can't remember what I dreamed about. But were you sure you didn't hear me Shouting? '

Jasmine said, "No, what did you dream about?"

It was still dark in the bedroom at 3a.m., and Mark, already scared, didn't want to add to his wife's fears. "I dreamed someone was calling for us, for both of us," he said.

Mark doesn't want to play up the horror in the dark, but his wife Jasmine says, "Do you often dream about killing people like this?"

"I really can't remember," Mark said. But I did have dreams about killing people a few times when I was a kid. When I was in primary school, I had three good friends whose parents were physics teachers in a middle school not far from the primary school. So when school was over at noon, we often went to play in the middle school, in the physics building. One night, I dreamed that I was in the hall of the physics building. The bronze statues and potted plants were exactly the same as in reality. I couldn't tell whether I was in a dream or in reality at all. Suddenly, I had a fight with someone, and with a flying kick I knocked his head off. The man's head rolled into the crevill between the statue and the potted plant, and his body fell beside me. I was afraid and ran into a wheat field. It became dark and I hid in a little hut in the wheat field. The fields were full of police cars, the police were searching, and the sirens pierced my eardrums. I saw red and blue police lights flashing and the cabin became like a house of horrors. I was scared to death."

Mark paused. Jasmine asked a curious question in a low voice, "So, were you afraid of killing someone, or were you afraid of being caught?"

Mark was a little surprised, thought for a while,

and replied, "Maybe you're afraid of getting caught."

Jasmine said, "I didn't expect it to be so long ago that you can remember it quite well."

Mark said, "Because it's scary. The fear was so real that even when I woke up, I thought I was in a dream. I don't know why I see red and blue light in my dreams. Maybe I remember something wrong."

The night was turned over. When the subject came up again the next day, Mark told Jasmine exactly what had happened in his dream. He told Jasmine that he didn't want her to feel more scared late at night. He didn't mean to cheat.

Mark loves his wife and is always honest with her. But like the dream at 3 a.m., there were many other visions popping up in Mark's mind. These visions are out of Mark's control at all times of the day and night, and almost all of them are terrifying, surprising and frightening to Mark himself. He did not dare to tell his wife, let alone anyone else, for fear that he would be seen as a horrible freak.

If the "self calling" scene in the dream can be explained as "the id undoing the previous cry for help," the visions popping up in Mark's head at any moment leave little room for explanation.

For example, when the cat knocks over the water glass, he will suddenly think of throwing the cat in the oven, or wring the cat's neck. If the family dog knocks over a trash can, he thinks of hanging it from a tree, cutting off its head with a knife, or shooting it into a cactus with a bow and arrow. There's also the illusion of shattering all the roofs with shotguns, or the illusion of shooting down moose with sniper rifles and pistols. Because these visions are based on real things, Mark feels a strong sense of empathy, almost like he's been in one of the scariest horror movies. Of course, that would have been all right if the vision had ended there, but in fact there were many more horrible visions, undescribable in their process, scenarios of hell on earth, of the end of the world. Mark knows that these are false, bad, and not to do, but the illusions still keep cropping up. Mark's belief in human nature becomes his last defense against all aggressive behaviors.

To prevent him from behaving badly, Mark imagines himself as a robot, with a red attack button placed on top of his head and covered by a hard glass cover. In the face of small, sudden and bad things, Mark mentally tells himself "don't judge an attack", "don't judge an attack", "don't judge an attack", which is not only saying don't judge the other party's action as an attack, but also telling himself not to produce any offensive action. Since the other party's behavior is not an attack on their own, then of course they do not need to retaliate, so do not and will not produce any offensive behavior. Mark relied on this method to get through a lot of restless days.

Mark's wife Jasmine is a physically and mentally healthy woman. Although she also has a variety of troublesome trivia and a lot of headaches, she is strong enough to face these problems and actively tries her best to solve them. In her eyes, her husband Mark is a loyal and reliable partner. Although he looks ordinary and even looks a little stupid, he is hardworking and can bear hardships, which is enough to shoulder the responsibilities of the family. But recently Mark has been a bit strange. He seems to have become dull. He often stands alone in a daze, frowning and thinking about something. If I asked, Mark just fobbed off and didn't elaborate. It seemed like he was trying to hide something. For some reason, Mark hadn't worked outside the home for a long time, so it wasn't clear what triggered Mark's mood change. And this change even often creates a textured atmosphere, like a dark mist that hangs around Mark and makes the people around him feel dull and depressing. Jasmine doesn't like that feeling, but she can't figure out the root cause of Mark's mood change, and she doesn't know how to solve this problem.

What's going on inside Mark?

III·Save Myself

The occurrence and onset of depression vary from person to person, and because it directly produces and acts on the body's soul container -- the brain, the causes of its onset are more elusive than those of any other organ in the human body. It can be said that we can generalize the causes of depression, but not the inductive factors of depression. People who like chilies find them delicious, while those who don't like them find them painful. It's the same with watching horror movies. People who like horror movies will find it a fun and exciting entertainment, while those who don't like horror movies will find it just asking for trouble.

In fact, when we look at the daily life, because of people's cognitive differences, many small things in life and work will also make people have different feelings and emotional changes. For example, couples who have just moved in together don't like put socks freely, can't stand the tip of a toothbrush being dropped into a mouthwash cup, or just want something that's neatly folded, whether it's towels or clothes. When these emotions continue to accumulate, and the person's mood is a bit sensitive and fragile, depression will take advantage of.

The world should be colorful as it is. If the world is full of warm love and tolerance, I think depression will be like mold in the sun, difficult to survive, or even won't exist at all. But unfortunately, light and dark always go together. It also makes me wonder: what role does depression play in the human world?

Of course, there are many patients who are physically and mentally healthy in their lives, but one day bad luck comes suddenly, or some unfortunate event happens suddenly, leading to a sudden surge of fear and anxiety, causing depression, and even "white hair overnight" occasionally.

If you fall into a state of depression, it is far better to help yourself in time than to wait for others to take the initiative to come to care and help.

Here, we mainly discuss how to achieve self-help in the self-destructing state of major depression by regulating their own psychological state. I'll leave it to the medical scientists and philosophers to argue about the nature of mental illness, as a perfectly normal human being, just trying to survive.

There is no logic to the methods listed here, and

there is no particular order. Just choose whichever method you like. If you're not sure where to start, try doing them one by one in numerical order.

Method 1) Drop Everything and Find Yourself

If you want to solve a mental illness, you may turn to psychology first. However, as a percentage of the total population on the planet, the number of people who practice and master psychological theories is tiny, and even fewer still end up doing it. Of course, I encourage and advise you to seek professional treatment if you can. Here, I would like to say some of my own views.

Understanding psychology is a good thing, but even if you have the theoretical knowledge of psychology, you may not be able to help yourself from the state of depression. The great psychology expert Mr. Jung, in the construction of his own psychological theory of the temple of the road, several times into a state of depression, his reason and state of mind almost collapsed, and finally with the help of friends just recovered. And the greater teacher of psychology, Mr. Freud, the psychological state of his life is not placid, to describe with turbulent waves is appropriate. So, if you don't know anything about psychology at all, don't worry, as far as I'm concerned, psychology is not the only way to achieve psychological self-help, the vast majority of people on this planet don't understand the theory of psychology, but you still have the opportunity and the method of self-help. Theory and knowledge are invaluable treasures in human civilization, but human beings are by no means completely dependent on these theories and knowledge to evolve to today. Ignorance is not so much a sin in terms of having a depressive mental illness alone. It's the first burden you need to let go.

On the other hand, human beings today do deserve to be at the top of the food chain above all other creatures, based on a system of civilization in which we are superior to other species. But if we look at it more broadly, outside of the human species itself, from the point of view of nature, we're just one of nature's creations. Humans can indeed claim to be at the top of the food chain, but it's hard to be specific about yourself. Because you're still more likely to become food than you are to eat your opponent when you're alone with lions, tigers and bears. It's neither a good thing nor a bad thing, it's an obvious and perfectly normal thing. By understanding this, you may be able to accept the fact that you are just a common creature in nature. Physical and mental strength is not strong, but it is normal, and this is the basic state of human beings when they return to nature, so that you can let go of the second burden.

Continue to think about it. If you are born as a lion, you face the fate of being banished from your family due to weakness. If you were born as a Wolf, you face a lonely fate of fighting for status or not fitting in with the rest of the pack. If you were born as a rabbit, then you have to face the fate of running and hiding and burrowing to save your life. If we look closely at these animals, we will see that they rarely complain about their lot. It would have been a hot topic if animal experts had had solid evidence to prove that they committed suicide because they didn't want to hide as a rabbit, or because they didn't want to kill as a lion. Some animals do behave like suicide, such as whales stranding and lemmings jumping into the sea, which we can't explain. In recent times, scientists have come up with explanations based on scientific observations and experiments. However, as a natural creature, people will choose suicide because they do not want to be human anymore, which is a very common mentality among people with major depression.

Don't be so quick to die. Let's analyze it again.

As we said, there are two things to put down. The two burdens, one is about ignorance, the other is about weakness. As I mull over the world, I find that the circumstances that force modern people into constant psychological despair are often implicitly linked to these two things. Each of us faces an external world that, because it prides itself on being civilized and efficient, is constantly forcing people to be omniscient and strong as iron in order to adapt to the high-intensity and high-stress work environment of our time. We have received all kinds of education from childhood, and we have seen all kinds of cruel competition in modern society. We seem to think that we should be omniscient and omnipotent, and we also feel that we should be as strong as iron. Unfortunately, our bodies and minds have not yet evolved into the structures needed for a modern, high-pressure society. You think you can do it. You think you should be able to do it. You think everyone else can do it, so you should be able to too. As everyone knows, in the face of such a society, the state of tolerating pressure is basically the same, but the inner state is different. Depression patients, is those who cannot bear the high intensity of pressure, but can not clearly see the state of the self, also difficult to face the self of those people.

The world expects you to contribute to its strength, the world expects you to contribute to its prosperity, and your boss expects you to overcome obstacles, learn to play the piano, and be an octopus-like multitasker juggling 100 high-octagon, everyday tasks. But I just want to ask a question: are you such a superman?

Again, to reiterate the theme, we're talking about self-help for people with major depression, we're not talking about inspirational stories.

So here, I want to continue to ask a few questions: Does the strength of society have anything to do with you? Does world peace have anything to do with you? Are all the boss's demands correct and reasonable? Even if you tried to work hard, could you evolve eight tentacles in your lifetime?

Dear reader, if you're arguing with me about the questions I just asked you, then congratulations, you're not suffering from major depression because you still have the sense and the mood to debate the obvious.

As a former sufferer of major depression, I want to say to you who are suffering from the same illness and mental dilemma: we are all ordinary creatures in nature, we are all ordinary people, we are not all-knowing gods, we are not steel robots. You are not missing in this world. But once you break down and take the initiative to end your life, your world is over. I don't know what you believe in, or whether you believe in the afterlife, but in my subjective judgment, your world is over. The earth is still spinning and the universe is still expanding. But your world, your universe, blew up and disappeared.

Have you ever thought about it? We came to this world, who are we? Why are we like this? What do we want to be? On the day when spring flowers bloom, we may poetically express that each flower carries its own mission. But will the flowers recognize our so-called poetic expressions? A plant, blooming in spring, is it really to bring color and fragrance to the world?

We are not so different from this flowering plant.

Let go of all this and find yourself. We are so unique, just like each flower in the flower field, seemingly identical to each other, but actually unique in the world, it is almost like some secret given to the world by God. Our uniqueness is the most fundamental attribute of our existence.

If it can't be done, it can't be done. If it doesn't work, it doesn't work. Say sorry to the world, and then look for those things that we can do, those things that we can accomplish, in this rich and colorful world, there is always something like this waiting for us to discover, waiting for us to accomplish.

Let those who are willing to challenge the

challenge to accept it, let those who are strong warriors to do their favorite struggle it. We are just ourselves, that's obvious.

Method 2) Slow Everything Down and Do Just a Little

With the development of modern times, everything seems to be connected with "fast and efficient", and "fast" has become a kind of positive measurement standard to evaluate human behavior.

From the 1950s, when China launched the "Great Leap Forward" and put forward the idea of "building socialism with more, faster, better and more economy", to the 1990s, when China put forward the idea that "time is money and efficiency is life", the whole society has been moving forward at a rapid speed like a crazy snowball.

Why is fast good? It's something I've been thinking about since I was a kid.

Even when people get together to cook during the Spring Festival, it is a matter of pride for them to make dumplings quickly.

I'm not criticizing these things, I'm just saying that perhaps our lives have slipped into a state of abnormally fast speed. Life has gone faster than normal, but we think it's normal. So much so that when we can't keep up with the speed, we think there is something wrong with ourselves.

In nature, farmers grow crops that do not grow faster because people want them to grow faster. They do not blossom and bear in February to satisfy the needs of farmers and all people. But modern people, simply like crops locked in a greenhouse, are completely confused about the season of growth, willfully grow, blossom and bear fruit, and strive to satisfy everyone's desire for fruit.

In the Eastern world, such as China, working overtime has become so common that special words like "996" and even "724" have been coined. Overwork and karoshi became the norm in Japan as early as the 1950s, and if a working man came home before 9 p.m., his wife became suspicious and worried about whether he had lost his job. I thought the Western world would be more rigorous about working time accounting, but when I see work emails being sent at 11pm and truck drivers driving down the highway at 100km/h while opening their laptops to attend Zoom conferences, I think the world has gone crazy.

If we go for "fast," we may one day evolve into annual herbs.

This "speed" can be particularly stressful for people in a state of depression.

My personal advice is to slow down. Reduce stress.

It's not just slowing down at work. I mean, when you're in a depressive state, everything slows down.

Think slowly. Walk slowly. Drink water slowly. Speak slowly.

I feel like I'm moving in water, and the air around me is holding me back. This resistance is not great, just enough to allow us to slowly lift our hands, get things done, and leave enough time to think about whether we need to do it, whether we have other options.

Extra stress can have unintended consequences that are difficult to understand and feel as a healthy person.

Of course, this is likely to affect people's productivity, because not all jobs allow people to slow down.

If you are already suffering from depression, please consider your work environment and take time off without too much hesitation when necessary. You are not a machine. You are not a slave. When your body and mind need rest and healing, this is normal and reasonable.

If you're in a work environment or work system that doesn't allow you to take time off or rest or therapy, you may want to consider leaving the environment. If you can't leave, you may want to consider deliberately reducing your productivity while keeping yourself safe. Do a little of everything, do your best, and never ask for too much.

I'm not telling you to cheat, but I'm saying that if a workplace or a social environment pursues its own interests and doesn't care about your health and safety, then why should you care about and love its interests? Is your life made for it? Are you a slave to it?

On the other hand, if I were the boss, pressing depressed employees to get their work done efficiently would be totally damaging to the enterprise. I will make an in-depth investigation into the causes of employees' emotional depression. If they are caused by the enterprise environment, I will try to make adjustments from the perspective of the enterprise environment.

I can only speak my thoughts and suggestions, my purpose is only to relieve the inner pressure of depression patients. In essence, this is a self-selecting question. Because I'm not sure, there may be people suffering from depression who are willing to speed up everything to get rid of their inner pain.

This is a self-help recommendation for people with major depression. It's not a doctor's order, nor is it a must.

Method 3) A Little Hope

To people who live a normal life, "hope" is like the air, always present in all directions, but we do not deliberately find it. It is not until our spirit is in some kind of desperate situation that we look for "hope" in the same way that our bodies are suffocated. But the worst of it is that in many cases our hearts really do cry out for help, longing for something so badly that we don't even know what it is that we are longing for until the end. This situation is vividly illustrated in The Last Leaf by The great short story writer O. Henry.

In desperation, we long for survival, our hearts long for salvation, and "hope" is the most important nourishment.

China's "People's Daily Online" once reported a news that a middle school teacher in Tianjin killed his daughter-in-law and hanged himself in prison after his couple went to the United States for reunion. This became a tragic tragedy. Carefully reading this story, we will find that the murderer had maintained great hope, but it was difficult to get along with each other because of the discord of ideas, and the last straw that broke the camel was his blocked exit. The old man had no way to enter, no way to retreat, so in anger and despair he attacked with his knife. If the victim can give a way out for them, all of they might still be able to survive. In these kinds of events, hope is often the rarest of keys.

For the mood has been in the state of depression of the individual, this "hope" is also the key to life, do not put all their retreat blocked. Mountains and rivers again suspected no road, and a village. If you stop at what seems like a dead end for a moment, get some fresh air and allow yourself to think for a minute more, you may find a new way out.

Where does our "hope" come from? When a great ship sinks, our hopes are directed towards the lifeboats, but without them we might as well use a life buoy, a life vest, or even a floating door or table. But all of these actions require the belief in our hearts that we are going to survive. That is the true source of hope.

If your heart is so heavy that you have lost this source of hope. I suggest you get up, stretch yourself, go for a hot cup of coffee, maybe some rum, but you don't need much hope, just a little. You do that, go for a five-minute walk, and when you come back, think again about hope.

You don't have to be right. You just need a little.

Hope is celebrated in many literary works, such as Stephen King's great works *The Shawshank Redemption* and *The Mist*, or in Mr. O 'Henry's short stories, such as *The Last Leaf*, or *Springtime A La Carte*, all extolling the preciousness of hope.

Not much, but just a little, enough to carry us through the darkness and oppression that temporarily enveloped our hearts until we stepped out into the wide, sunny world.

Method 4) Make small changes

Our daily life will actually have some small changes, it happens in every detail of our life. It's just that we didn't make these changes on purpose, so we didn't notice them. If you deliberately observe the way we use a mouse, for example, you will see that every time we hold the mouse, our bodies are subconsciously adjusting our movements. If we don't adjust properly, after a while, we develop a nasty condition called "mouse hand" or "carpal tunnel syndrome."Don't worry, it's both preventable and curable. I'm just illustrating how small changes can happen in our lives.

Our inner mood is also undergoing small changes every day, which is closely related to the new things we need to face every day. Lottery grand prize, can be happy for a long time, only picked up 1 yuan on the ground, can also be happy a small. All of these events trigger emotional reactions that, when combined, form the backbone of our mood over time and form the source of information for the basic ideas we form about an event, a person or a place. The world out there is so exciting that people who work outside the home are less likely to develop depression. People who work from home need to deliberately design small changes in their lives to prevent their moods from developing depressive symptoms when they are faced with both the lack of fresh and interesting input and the equally heavy stress of work.

Well, no matter where you work or live, if you are feeling depressed for some reason, you can try these methods.

For example, do you like flowers? Put some flowers on your desk. Whether it's dandelion or hyacinth collected by the side of the road, or sky star or carnation bought at the florist, it's a good choice. You might want a heavy container, but obviously a pot isn't that good. Try using square, thick-bottomed glasses, or clay jars. Cut the stems short and place them directly in these thick containers for stunning results.

A Transformers or Lego model is also a good choice. These things can move, they can change, they can change from day to day, just like those brief flowers that let us see something different on our desks every day, that tells us that today is different than yesterday.

Of course, if your desk is already overcrowded, how about getting a new keyboard once in a while? Would you like a heavy metal keyboard instead? Or a retro typewriter keyboard? Pink Hello Kitty, why not?

It's not a big deal if you can't be bothered to change the keyboard. Have you ever considered giving yourself a funny catchphrase? If you never used to just say, "Yes, boss," try saying, "Yeah, boss, Yeah."You don't like "yeah"? It's okay. Pick whatever you like. It's OK to say 'Darth Vader.' "Yes, boss, Darth Vader."Just go about your business and don't worry about the boss's face. Oh, if you're the boss, well, never mind the facial expressions of your employees. Life is so boring and depressing, why don't we change it a little to make it more interesting?

All it takes is a little change, a little change. If you don't like words, design a hand gesture for yourself. This month it's finger snapping, next month it's hand clapping. Don't scare others, but you can entertain yourself. That's enough.

On a personal level, it takes courage to make changes in any area, even when you decide to shave every day or wear lipstick every day. It takes some mental courage. But when our minds are healthy and strong, they are not worth talking about. But when our hearts are depressed and troubled, they sometimes need to be fought for. People who have never been in a state of depression, it is very difficult to experience this mood.

Don't worry, it's normal. Take your time. Just a little.

Method 5) Start a Business that Pleasures You

In modern society, it seems that it is not easy to start your own business, no matter what country you are in. In the end, those who are blessed with unique resources are in the minority. As ordinary people, we have to go through the road of entrepreneurship is often particularly difficult.

What we're talking about here is not the kind of entrepreneurship that ultimately leads to business success, social status, and financial freedom. Our fundamental goal is to get rid of psychological depression, so what we are talking about here is to pry open the shackles of the mind and break through the wall of depression. The only thing you have to do is please yourself.

To borrow the term "startup," what it really means here is just finding something to do for yourself. The reason we use the word "startup" is that we are looking for something that is not similar to what we are already doing, something that we are not used to doing. From this perspective, the word "startup" is not an understatement.

There are a few principles to follow when looking for your own startup.

First beginning is not too difficult. We just need to find something new to do. Don't beat yourself up. It's time to change the perception that entrepreneurship is a business that succeeds only through hard work. For us, starting something new just a little bit is a startup.

Creating a vehicle that can travel through time is a great venture, of course, but planting seeds and starting to grow plants is a great venture for someone who has never worked in agriculture."Difficult" and "easy" are very subjective feelings. For ballet dancers, high leg lifts are easy, but for the general public, who lack flexibility training, they are more difficult movements. Therefore, what kind of project to choose, difficult and easy to choose according to their own feelings. If you choose to relax by proving Goldbach's conjecture, it's commensurate, but if you choose to simply stand there and try to challenge yourself to the longest standing trance possible, it's also fine. In short, don't be hard on yourself, just choose what you like.

Second, we can continue to do it. If we want to start a career, but it's too short, we may not be able to reach the effect of depression. For example, we want to go to the supermarket and buy crisps from all brands as a business that we want to start. In theory, there is no problem at all, but in practice, it seems too short. Go to the snack area of the supermarket, soon bought out. Perhaps it is the ambition to buy every brand of crisps in every supermarket in the country that makes this challenging. If you really decide to do it, it's fine. Don't worry too much about other people's eyes, just be happy. I can illustrate the problem of persistence with an example of playing cards. If you want to use poker to relieve depression, call friends to play naturally is the best, only their own words, you can try to practice shuffling.

Following the "not too hard" principle, we don't need to practice to the level of a casino dealer, just do a smooth two-handed stack shuffle, or simply shuffle the deck. If you find yourself with a good hand, challenge yourself to a more difficult move. As we explained earlier, hard and easy are very subjective feelings. If you have a good hand with a poker shuffle, a move that seemed difficult at first will now look easier as your skill improves. If you still have a mediocre hand or just aren't interested in shuffling cards, you can also try flying cards, which is the kind of action you see in videos where you use cards as darts to fly. It may be difficult at first, but the skill will get better and better with practice. By "persistence" I mean the process shown in the example above. Whatever you do, make it as simple and relaxing as possible for a while.

The third is to obtain "growth pleasure". At the beginning of the writing and the title of this section is set to "start a boring career", I mean to start the business does not need special significance, also is not a business success and, for the purpose of achieving personal social value is purely his be fond of, or just to kill time, to eliminate depression. In fact, if you think about it carefully, everything is based on national, social and other people's standards to do things, this is the most boring, right? Can we even say that this is the source of psychological stress, is it the "original sin" that produces depression? Every person in this world has a unique personality, each person's face is different, how can you achieve the same standard? Isn't it hypocritical to dream together? Pleasing yourself is the most meaningful thing in the world.

Going back to the text, the laws of cosmic physics tell us that energy is conserved and that whatever you do for it will always earn you something interesting in return. For example, in the case of flying cards we just mentioned, if you practice them over and over again, the cards will actually cut the fruit and open the cans like darts. This is a skill that gets stronger with practice. Or imagine if someone actually decided to buy every brand of crisps available in supermarkets across the country, using social media platforms to record their progress. Maybe it will become some kind of commercial selling point? Something accumulates, more and more and more and more and more and more and more and more and more and more and more, and this is one of the sources of lasting human happiness.

I am now writing incessantly, which is a way of starting my own boring business. I love writing, even though the financial rewards are almost nil. But if I persist, my ability to think, tell stories, and write will improve, won't I? It's hard for me to write when I'm depressed, but it's also true that I don't feel depressed when I'm writing, and for that reason alone, I'm happy to keep writing. I bought myself a new used keyboard, put my coffee and handheld game next to my laptop, and if I'm in a good mood, think seriously about what I'm going to write next. Reading about the experiences shared by people with mental illness, you will find that "writing it down" can be a great tool for self-therapy. There's no clinical data to back it up, so it's probably a very personalized approach. And the so-called "write down", also does not need to write like me tens of thousands of words, only need a simple to write some thoughts, feelings, thoughts, bit by bit to write, but also comb their own thoughts, bit by bit to know one's own soul, just like to look in the mirror one's own soul, may be able to finally realize to save itself. This is the same as the " Confront It Bravely: Exhale the Devil's Name" method below.

There are many similar careers to choose from, such as hand knitting, crocheting, knotting, making key chains, telling stories, recording short videos, drilling for wood for fires, accumulating readings, picking up coins, drawing, practicing calligraphy, learning a new language, and so on. It's never too late to start. I don't expect anything from it anyway. The greatest success is to please myself and relieve the depression in my heart.

Method 6) Chat: Keep Your Message Diverse

I can fully understand that if a depressed patient has an attack and is in a state of severe depression, it is also difficult to ask the patient to have a daily chat with others. But in terms of relieving depression, talking is definitely a good way to do it.

Chatting is one of the most fun ways to open up quickly, and getting together with a couple of friends for a chat is definitely one of the happiest moments in life. Stress borne alone multiplies geometrically, and stress shared with others diminishes geometrically. Chatting, piled up in our heart trouble and anguish of vent out, all at the same time we also share other people's stories, anecdotes and pressure of these our joy and pain to each other closely together in life, let each of us received a group symbiotic sense of security, and been accepted by the group approval by happiness. You see, this is what a pleasant process!

If we look at chat from the perspective of human brain feedback and processing, we can see that it can even be a lifesaver.

Chat for a life? Exactly. Are you kidding me? You'll see.

It starts with the concept of "Gaslighting." The gaslight effect is a form of psychological manipulation that first appeared in the 1938 American stage play Gas Light. The release of film adaptations of the same name in 1940 and 1944 helped popularize the concept of the "gaslight effect" and made it a defining term in social fields as diverse as clinical psychology, political commentary, and philosophy. What is it specifically? That is, by questioning the normal reactions and thoughts of the controlled person, distorting the normal value judgment of the controlled person, implanting the value judgment set by the controlled person, implanting the reward and punishment switch, and finally realizing the psychological manipulation of the controlled person. If you search for the term "Gaslighting," you'll find a number of startling things, from individual crimes to the actions of states. The Gaslighting effect appears and reappears in all sorts of events, large and small.

Typical uses of the "gaslight effect" to carry out crimes include: cults, pyramid schemes, Internet addiction treatment centers, Blue Whale death games, Internet telecom fraud, and so on. In the course of investigating these crimes, we often see descriptions such as, "confiscated mobile phones, cut off the couple from the outside world; Lock the door of the "home" and prohibit the couple from leaving, depriving the couple of their personal freedom; Forced to leave the new people in the pyramid selling hideout, continuous door-to-door brainwashing, and beat the new people who do not cooperate ", the criminals will first isolate the victims to the information island, and then forced to distort their normal judgment, and finally achieve psychological control. What if you can't distort the victim's normal judgment? They will kill the victim. If you look up the Beijing News report on October 23, 2019, "College student was duped to death in pyramid scheme 15 years ago" or "Li Wenxing incident," you can see a detailed description of the case. The infamous "Blue Whale Death Game", which began in Russia, is an avid user of the "Gaslight Effect". If we're looking for more, we'll find Pauline Dakin, who lives in Canada and has a life as strange as an alien encounter, with a gaslight hanging over her head. The process was captured in her autobiography, Run, Hide, Repeat: A Childhood Memoir of Escape. A Memoir of A Fugitive Childhood, which won the 2018 Edna Staebler Award for Creation in Non-Fiction. If you're interested, you can search and read it for yourself. It's absolutely creepy.

Today, the Gaslight Effect has been reinvented

as the "PUA Pick-Up Artist," and it's as sleazy as it gets. It also makes me particularly amazed at the fragility of the human soul.

Back to the title, chat for life, is based on the above kinds of psychological control behavior. Watch these crimes, we can discover, offender want to control others, first have to cut off the victim's information communication channels, regardless of the offenders "what banner, adopt what means, to say something nice, or ugly word is cut off victim of information exchange and communication with the outside world, monopoly victim source of information. Some victims caught up in cults and pyramid schemes have been rescued because they have made contact with the outside world through their courage and wit. If you don't fall into this information island, if you talk to people regularly, if you talk to strangers regularly, if you learn a lot of new information, if you keep diversifying the information in your head, I think you'll almost never fall into this criminal trap, and that's what I mean by "saving lives by talking."

Here, I'd like to share some of my personal conversation tips to avoid the embarrassment of not knowing what to talk about when we make eye contact with our friends, colleagues, and neighbors. What to talk about and with whom, the details are as follows.

First, talk to living people. Family and friends are great, of course, but co-workers are great, neighbors are great, and strangers are necessary. We live in different environments, access to information in a variety of ways, so that we have a rich source of information. Just as our bodies need elemental nourishment to survive, our souls also need information nourishment to survive. The gaslight effect works because we are cut off from information, the fuel of the soul. If you eat a single food, you become malnourished, and the same is true of the soul, which receives only one piece of information. When the soul is malnourished, it loses the information basis for facts, value judgments, and self-judgment, and it becomes very easily controlled by others. Therefore, from this perspective, we can find that strangers may be more valuable for chatting, because strangers will give us more fresh information. What on earth? Let's talk about the weather. Start with the weather. If there's nothing else to talk about after the weather, move on to someone else. It's as simple as that.

Let's talk about chatting from the perspective of information digestion and acceptance. We can imagine chatting with others as a plant: chatting with strangers is equivalent to the plant's leaves getting sunshine and rain; Chatting with neighbors, equivalent to chlorophyll into energy, has become the basic consensus in a small range of people; Chatting with friends is equivalent to sharing energy and nutrients, making plants of the same kind grow and thrive together. By talking to family members, the plant is reinforcing its roots.

Of course, this metaphor takes place when chatting and information transfer are particularly smooth. If we compare the common situation encountered by Mr. Lao She during the "Cultural Revolution" in China, father and son become enemies and husband and wife become enemies, chatting may turn into some deadly behavior. Which brings me to why I say "talk to the living"? Is it possible to talk to the dead as well as to the living? Yes. We need to talk to the dead, and it's a great way to get information.

Second, talk to the dead. There was a book called Postmortem by Patricia Cornwell, an American author, which fascinated me. To be honest, the content is nothing new, but the straightforward title, "Bodies Talk," intrigued me. It seems to me that the dead speak all the time, only not in the way we are accustomed to imagine, but in the form of last words, in short, books. Read Shakespeare's plays, but the great Shakespeare is long dead, his soul remains in the book, to tell us what he saw and thought. Read the works of Mr. Stephen King. Mr. Stephen is still alive, but a part of his soul has been in his works forever, telling us what that part of his soul saw and thought. Read them. That's what I mean by "talking to the dead."I'm being sensational, and you could say that while you were reading this book, you were talking to my soul. Exactly. I hope you read more books. Any how, also don't have to read every book, of course, don't have to read every word, but the more you read, the more you get information of the well-documented, you'll have a more reliable basis of the information, again and again, finally you will be able to get your own solid facts, value and personal judgment standard, your soul will also in the continuous reading is becoming more and more strong. Forgive me for calling reading "talking to the dead," but if you look at the prevalence of horror stories throughout human history and the total disregard and contempt for reading by billions of people around the world, you can probably understand my sensationalism. Besides, I'm a horror writer myself, and I love it.

Third, talk to yourself. When you're talking to friends and family, and you're reading, don't forget to listen to your own voice, the voice that comes from within. You're human yourself, aren't you? When you are in despair, or accidentally trapped in an island of information, don't forget to listen to your own voice. Your hopes, your demands, and your fears will all emerge as you sit quietly and listen to yourself. It's an important way to help yourself if you're depressed. When you have enough information, you can also construct your own world inside, you will have more ways to save yourself, your soul will be strong enough to resist the "gaslight effect" and the stupid and evil PUA, and depression will be overcome. This is a process full of hardships but also full of light to find themselves.

Finally, I want to mention a very dangerous island of information. This danger extends to everyone within the information island, and of course to everyone who mentions it, so I need to speak out carefully. Human beings are small, especially individuals. When our thoughts are at the national level, we may feel that we have the eyes to see the world, but we do not. People who think this way, I call them shortsighted, arrogant, and complacent. In reality, even a country with more than a billion people can be a huge island of information. Only people in the isolated island, believe a certain thought, only believe some people's speech, and willing to will be taught these ideas as their own point of view, refused to accept the new information, proud to adhere to the dogma, rubbish and all in the name of the great glory to make a lot of harm, the loss of human nature of crimes, until the crime itself, You are foolish and do not know how to repent. This does not happen only in one country, nor in one form of reality, but their essence is the same.

In my opinion, the only way to break these silos of information is through the three approaches we have discussed above. Not only can it relieve depression, but chatting can sometimes be lifesaving.

Method 7) Find Amulets

Although we don't live in a magical world, amulets are really important things. If your heart is always in a state of fear, lack of necessary security, the soul in a long-term fear, then you cannot lift the state of depression. In such cases, you can consider wearing an amulet, which will greatly help you to restore your sense of security.

By amulet, I don't mean something that you have to go to a temple, a church, a synagogue, or a mosque to get. You don't need to search for holy water or excavate an unknown Inca imperial temple of the sun to get it. Think about it. If you had an older brother or sister who was strong enough to make you feel secure, would they have run out from the ancient temple of Machu Picchu to protect you?

I found a few items, listed below, and you can

choose any you like. Or, if you like, choose any of them. I only provide ideas. You have to prepare the stuff yourself. The only thing that suits you best is what you prepare yourself.

The list is as follows:

A headset. A tactical pen. A whistle. A flashlight. A Cross. Sunglasses. Toy guns. Bullet cases. A baseball cap. A ruler. A comb. A short stick. A wooden block. LEGO bricks.   Hair clips. Necklaces. A ring. Bracelets. Ankle rings. A phone pendant. Stickers. Badges. Holy water. A carry-on flask.   Icons. Bible. A tattoo. A doll. A candy. Small stones. A small mirror. A leaf. A branch. Mysterious bark. Origami. Resin puppies. Woodcut toys. A crayon. A photo. A mini book. A key chain. Earplugs. A song. A melody. A word. A spell. A poem. A small gesture. A color. A shape. Mysterious content written by yourself.

In addition, there are some items with a unique style. Some people like to carry cleaned chicken bones with them, others monkey feet, rabbit feet, goat ears or black donkey hooves, and even human ashes, like Kuman Thong, or dried human heads, For Tsantsa or Tzantza or Shrunken Head, all I can say is, "OK, whatever makes you happy."

But when it comes to carrying items of "talisman" significance, I think it's important to follow a few simple rules. In the end, these items are not extraordinary.

My rule is this: I choose a "talisman" item that fits in a pocket, fits in one hand, doesn't have a sharp edge, and doesn't produce a distinctive sound, light or smell. This is the best choice.

If a man walks through the crowd with a gun or a

machete in order to feel safe, the image must be very unsettling to the people around him. If a person makes the people around him feel insecure, does he really feel safe? I don't think so. So it's important to make others feel as safe and secure as you feel safe and secure in yourself.

Whatever you do, try to create a sense of security in your life, especially your inner security.

No matter in which country, under which civilization system, if long-term lack of security, people will certainly become beasts, even demons.

Method 8) Engage in "Heavy Physical Labor"

By "heavy physical work" we are not talking specifically about work in agriculture or industry, for example, but work that requires the full capacity of your body. If you can, you can farm for a while, move building materials around a construction site, etc., but if you're not the kind of athlete who exercises regularly, I don't recommend that you start out with heavy physical labor. I recommend jumping rope, leg lifts in place, fist swinging and other ways to open up your body's motor function.

Everyone's physical condition is different, and the term "heavy manual labor" needs to be discussed in terms of each person's physical condition. We are not going to be sent to "labor" criminals (" labor ", dubbed "the People's Republic of China" only a handful of countries have this words, is not is about to take part in sports game "professional athlete" (" professional athlete ", this also is only a few countries have unique words, I use these two words, because they are mandatory, requiring you to meet a certain amount of labor or exercise prescribed by a leader to be qualified, they add to the horror of the term "hard physical labor."

So why do I have to use the phrase "hard physical labor" here? It's because we need to distinguish the kind of labor or movement that we're doing at this time from the kind of activity that we normally do, that requires a little bit of hard work. For us to alleviate the state of depression as the goal, according to their own situation to adjust the amount of exercise, is the most suitable state.

For a long time engaged in heavy lifting industry workers, their new bought TV into the house, should be an easy thing. But for people who have long been clerical in the office and don't get much exercise, it can be hard, heavy manual work. So for people who have been depressed for a long time, maybe getting out of the house is a physical labor to some extent. This is the level at which we need to understand the individual differences in the term "heavy manual labor."

However, the objective fact is also clear, even if we understand the psychological level of the "heavy physical" difference, but just walking out of the house, it is very difficult to "heavy physical" spending, it can only be regarded as breaking the shackles of the psychological, although commendable, but not enough. Our body is a vessel for the soul, and the weakness of the soul is often closely related to the weakness of the body. In Doraemon's story, Nobita will be afraid of many small things, while Pagato is willing to challenge the unknown, which has something to do with the psychological confidence brought by his strong body. If we want to quickly improve the psychological condition, produce a more obvious effect, exercise body is a very good way. Of course, just getting out of the house doesn't count, you need to do more than that.

Other behaviors that don't count include walking around the room, simple gymnastics, climbing stairs at a constant speed, simple limb movements, shaking your head, typing fast, mouse-clicking furiously, and so on.

The "heavy physical labor" we need requires your body to do relatively intense activities in a short period of time. Anaerobic exercise should be relatively intense, aerobic exercise should be relatively lasting, and your body will feel slightly tired at the end of the exercise, which is a better state. It's okay to increase the amount of exercise or work you're expected to do because you feel good about your body. Just be sure to exercise safely, and try not to go too far beyond your current physical limits, as that could lead to Rhabdomyolysis or other injuries.

Remember our goal? We're just trying to improve depression, so moderate amounts of "heavy energy" exercise are always best. Personally, I highly recommend the Burpee, which works about 70% of the muscles of the whole body, including the core muscles, feet, waist, back, hands and hips. The specific action can be searched on the Internet, and find the one that suits you. Be sure to remember, we are not professional athletes, and we are not participating in the competition, so it is not important to have very standard movements, as long as the whole thing is similar, and gradually get closer to the standard. Don't do too many bobbies at first. Personally, I recommend doing 5 to 10 Burpee in groups and resting immediately after each group is finished. How many sets do you do each day, depending on your mood. The nice thing about Burpee is that it doesn't emphasize the field as much, and it doesn't make any extra sound. You can start practicing anytime, anywhere, and it's all under your own control. You can do this outdoors in a safe place, or quietly in your bedroom. This is the important reason why I love Burpee.

In addition, I also recommend rope skipping, frog jumping, leg raising, boxing, yoga, etc. The principles of exercise are the same as the basic principles of poppy jumping above. We are not athletes, we have to do it our way.

Oh, and remember the title of this section? Engage in "heavy physical labor". Burpee is called a "sport" rather than a "labor" because we can't make a product out of it. If we put a kinetic energy conversion device under our feet and generate electricity for our house by performing the Burpee, Burpee would go from "movement" to "labor" in an instant. In essence, our bodies do the same thing, but work may attract us even more than exercise, giving us the "thrill of growth."So, if you decide to start pulling weeds in your backyard, tilling the soil, or even starting a porter's job, it will be perfect.

Method 9) Confront It Bravely: Exhale the Devil's Name

Now let me ask a question: when we face the highwayman, we and the highwayman are very afraid, we are afraid of being hurt by the highwayman, so what is the highwayman afraid of?

In my opinion, gangsters are most afraid of being seen by us. When we recognize the gangster, write down the appearance of the gangster, then the possibility of the gangster being brought to justice to accept legal sanctions is greatly improved, so the gangster is most afraid of being recognized by us. That's why highwaymen often wear masks.

For our inner gangster, the loathsome depression and its complications, there is also a fear of recognition. Or maybe it's because we don't recognize these symptoms, and it's hard to see what's going on inside us, that the onset of depression becomes so crazy.

Continued depression, feelings of lack of happiness, emptiness, exhaustion, loss of worth, lack of self-confidence, and thoughts of suicide are typical symptoms of depression.

Nervous, unable to relax, constantly worried that something bad is going to happen, all kinds of terrible things and terrible outcomes are constantly rolling in the mind, this is anxiety, is a manifestation of insecurity, but also associated with depression symptoms.

Always wanting to check the door lock, always wanting to check the gas, always wanting to check the faucet, always wanting to be extra polite to others, always fearing that things will not be done properly. This is an obsessive-compulsive disorder, a lack of confidence, and a concomitant symptom of depression.

It's a symptom of paranoia and mania, and in some cases a concomitant symptom of depression, to feel that everyone around you is stupid, so weak and so weak that you want to stomp them to death.

For more detailed behavioral information, see the second part of the book, "Depression from multiple perspectives," or read the results of professional research on depression.

For us suffering from depression, do not escape, do not have to be afraid, when we recognize these symptoms, we should speak out in the first time, exhale the name of these demons. Can say to others, also can say to oneself, in short, do not escape. Most cases of mental illness are not the patient's fault, and I can tell you with a good grace that I have had it, and that's fine. Perhaps one day the disease recurred, I will not hesitate to face the devil.

Other methods are more manipulative, such as putting your inner feelings on the tip of a pen, finding a random notebook and writing them down. Not only write about it, but come back often so that you can see where your soul is and what it looks like, and it will be relatively easy to see problems, as mentioned in Method 5) Start a Business that Pleasures You. This is a self-executing process of demonic discovery.

If we cannot face the devil, it is very difficult for us to defeat him.

We can see this in The movies The Exorcist, Constantine, Hellboy, The Last Exorcism, Cleansing Hour and many other television and artistic works. The Exorcist motivates The ritual and confirms The identity of The devil. They then exclaim the demon's name during a purification ritual to send the demon back to hell. Demons, however, do not sit still. They fight back and make their names long and complicated. The higher the demon, the longer its name becomes, making it difficult for exorcists who cannot learn RAP to send the demons back to the hell. Fortunately, "depression" is just one word.

Here, I want to say a special case. Let's say we find someone around us who occasionally has a depressive episode but quickly returns to normal, or goes back and forth but always returns to normal. In this case, don't try to tell the person about the depression, and don't try to intervene when the person is depressed. Just gently talk them out.

In severe depression, calling out the devil's name can help us face it and fight it out. Under mild depression, once call out the demon's name, and sometimes it will aggravate. Leave it alone maybe is the better way to go.

Method 10) Discover the Infinite Possibilities in Life

When I was searching for all kinds of interesting stories, I found Mr. Ge Yulu. His performance art was very interesting. The most famous is the "Ge Yulu Incident".

Baiziwan Nan Yi Road in Beijing's Chaoyang District was named in 2005 and the road signs were put in place in time. However, because the management right of a small part of the road has not been handed over to the Beijing municipal government for the time being, so there is no road sign in this part of the road, so Mr. Ge Yulu made a road sign with his own name, "Ge Yulu Road", and installed it on this road by himself. This was the beginning of the "Ge Yulu Incident" in 2013.Of course, the Beijing municipal authorities wouldn't approve Mr. Ge's installation of street signs. He did it on the sly. But the most interesting part is that since Mr. Ge installed the street signs, operating in China Gaode, Baidu's navigation map network service providers such as approved by the road, have to add in their own electronic map database, and the traffic police in Beijing ticket to peccancy vehicles on the road, will also place written as double Wells street Ge Yulu road, Beijing municipal authorities also numbered the street lamps along the road with the name Ge Yulu. It was not until Ge graduated in 2017 that the incident was finally discovered and quickly went viral on the

Internet. It was not until the relevant government departments realized that they seemed to have been tricked that the sign was removed on July 13, 2017, along with the abolition of the road name. Mr. Ge completed a very interesting performance art experiment with his own effort. He is a master's student majoring in experimental art.

In addition, when Mr. Ge was a student, there are some very interesting performance art, such as he once secretly removed the bus stop sign of Beijing Donghu Station, and then transported to Wuhan, installed on the water surface of Wuhan Donghu Lake. He was disciplined on the day before his graduate school graduation for installing a dildo on top of the national flag pole. Or he climbed the scaffolding and looked into the eyes of hundreds of millions of cameras across China. In addition to Mr. Ge's interesting soul, I also seriously suspect that he also has some kind of special family background. In China, such acts are enough to land ordinary people in jail for a long time.

When you are depressed and unable to feel happy, does it make you feel any fun to see all the strange things this funny Mr. Ge does?

Serious life, rigorous style, work seriously, meticulous people, especially prone to depression and depression. Nervousness and anxiety encourage them to maintain a consistent cautious style, which in turn deepens the depression. When we observe Mr. Ge's behavior under this mood, do we feel a little strange? Mr. Ge took his artistic work seriously, meticulously doing useless things that made people feel weird and ridiculous. This is similar to the way we take our life and work seriously, meticulously doing what we think is full of significance, which may seem strange and ridiculous to outsiders, but we are unaware of it.

This is the value of performance art, by observing Mr. Ge's strange behavior, we can also see our own behavior to a certain extent.

So relax a little and stop suppressing your feelings for what you think is meaningful. If you already know that what you're doing doesn't matter, it's not worth taking it seriously. Of course, this should only be used to alleviate depressive symptoms, not as an excuse for slacking off. To you, feeling is absolute, but to the world as it exists, feeling is relative. The world is inherently unfair, but your respect and seriousness to the world still have a chance to earn the world's respect and seriousness for you.

In Ge Yulu's case, we may also be able to see the infinite possibilities in life. First ask yourself a question, who does the world belong to? Wang Shouren, a famous philosopher in the Ming Dynasty, said, "When you do not see the flower, the flower and your heart are silent. When you look at the flower, the color of the flower becomes clear to you. You will know that the flower is not in your heart."", that is, the so-called "heart outside unreasonable, heart outside nothing", I think can be put here as an answer.

As independent individuals of objective existence, it is indeed difficult for us to confront this magnificent world which is also objective existence. But, if we leave this world, we will no longer feel its existence. Then, for ourselves, the so-called objective existence of the grand world is also disappeared. From this perspective, who does the world belong to? Your own world, all your own.

Life is always infinite possibilities, let us in our own world, with a happy mood to try, slowly discover the countless possibilities of life.

Method 11) Drink Some Wine

It has been widely recognized and accepted that different foods can change one's mood. Professional studies have shown that eating protein can improve the body's alertness, while eating carbohydrates can reduce stress. Foods that have a significant impact on our mood, such as chocolate, bananas, crisps and cake, can make us feel the magic effect of mood change in the moment we eat. Search for "MOOD FOOD," and we'll find the results of a lot of professional research on the Internet.

The idea that food changes your mood is entirely based on the body's nature as a "biochemical factory". Just as the scent of a flower makes us happy, and the smell of feces makes us get away, so the soul produces different emotional responses to the food our body processes in this "biochemical factory."

Chocolate does have soothing effects, but for an even more relaxing effect, try drinking a little alcohol.

If common food is nourishment for the body, wine is nourishment for the soul.

Wine can relieve the fatigue of physical workers, relax the tension of mental workers, shorten the distance between strangers, increase the intimacy between friends, let the painful and melancholy soul temporarily forget the sadness, and have a certain probability to catalyze beautiful and moving poetry.

There are hundreds of different types of wine, with a wide range of flavors, which makes it a good hobby to study.

Wine is also closely related to the development of human history. In major historical events, traces of wine can often be found. Perhaps a cup of wine, you have tasted the desert sand two thousand years ago alone.

The drinking age is strictly regulated by law to protect overall human health.

In addition, I know that many religious laws prohibit alcohol consumption. No offense, I respect all laws and doctrines and follow them.

Method 12) Start Singing

There was a time when my life was very boring, getting up, surfing the Internet, reading books, eating and sleeping. This situation lasted about 2 to 3 months, and did not feel anything wrong at that time, but there was always a feeling of inexplicable irritability in my heart. Until one day, I inadvertently found a mix of pop songs on the Internet. When the music played, my heart seemed to feel the spring rain moisten, so I listened to it crazily for several hours, from which I fully realized Mr. Bai Juyi's "never hear the sound of bamboo and filigreed for year" and suddenly heard the complex mood of pipa music. Since then, I have resumed the hobby of listening to music.

That's right, recovery. In my depression, I completely forgot about listening to the music.

Music can affect people's mood, beautiful melodies can soothe the pain of the soul.

Elegant and moving singing is the pain of the depressed life.

We can not only listen, but also sing together. Even if there is no sound, there is no problem at all. No one gave us a penny anyway, so what difference did it make if we sang well?

If you check the Internet, you can even find articles on "Six Great Benefits of Singing." These include: lower high blood pressure, prevent dementia, help you burn fat, feel good about yourself, help you release oxytocin, exercise your mouth muscles, and more. More rigorous scientific research on the "function of music" is showing us how music affects our thoughts, moods, and psychological states, showing us that beautiful music can indeed nourishing our souls.

The moment I rediscovered my love of listening to music, I was reminded of The scene in *The Shawshank Redemption* in which Andy plays The aria *Canzonetta sull'aria* on The phonograph in The warden's office to The entire prison. The west wind is soft, blowing over my heart, beautiful and mind-boggling. It was a small but enduring tribute to freedom and hope.

Method 13) Soul Doll: Have a Meeting with Yourself

As discussed above, we already know that fresh information plays an important role in personal mental growth and maintenance of mental health, but sometimes we have to face the lack of new information, as well as some more special situations: even with new information, we still cannot control the drastic changes in our emotions. This is when we need a more powerful form of self-control: meetings with ourselves. It's not a fancy name, but it's just to make the method easier to understand.

In a nutshell, the core of this method is "splitting the self."I must emphasize that what I mean by "split self" is completely different from the psychiatric disorders such as "schizophrenia", "multiple personality" and so on. Also, it's something I've been using myself, and it's kept me sane, but I'm not sure it works for other people.So be sure to read what I've described carefully before you decide if you want to try it yourself.

Regarding outbursts, we can assume that an event model: we all know, one in their right mind would not casually indulgence to show emotion, especially in public, but also need to consider the scene atmosphere, each other's face, implied, the ways of the world as the basis of their words and deeds to play it by ear. People who are able to be flexible and versatile are praised as having a high EQ. What if someone is not emotionally intelligent and is prone to emotional outbursts? If his leader is present, he can be repressed with power. If the leader is not there, there may be a respected person to suppress; if there is no one of high esteem, there will be someone close to that person to comfort; if you do not even close to the people, there may be a kind-hearted simple people to comfort. All of the people mentioned above, sometimes at the same time, sometimes alone. If none of them show up, surrounded by people who look at jokes, and the external environment is completely indifferent, then this person with low emotional intelligence will probably actually explode, and maybe cause some trouble, maybe lead to a tragedy. The so-called "low EQ" here is just a relative concept. Things are difficult and hearts vary, and the level of EQ is just a simple description. In fact, it is a variable that is difficult to grasp. Some people steal dishonest slippery, cheap take, seemingly EQ is very low, but meet the need for "good human nature" of the situation, but very understand the truth of wisdom to protect oneself, this EQ instant on the high up. Some people diligent, kind-hearted simple, but encounter the mother was raped nowhere to avenged, but also by the mob to the door of the situation, may choose the kind of "you don't give me a statement, I will give you a statement" extreme emotional vent way. You'll have to judge for yourself.

If we observe this event model, we will find that,

in fact, there are so many people to help a person suppress or relieve his emotional outburst before he loses control. It is only when the whole external environment is completely indifferent that he will finally break out. This is the rationale for what I call a "meeting with yourself" approach. The main purpose of using this method is to conduct self-help guidance and control of my emotions when my emotions are difficult to control and the external environment is completely indifferent. The starting point of this approach is our desire to continue to lead a normal life.

How does it work?

When we're emotionally out of control and in need of catharsis, there's no time to grab the boss and bully ourselves. What should I do? We split a boss-like self from our consciousness to suppress. If you're a rebel and want to punch your boss when he's overriding you, try splitting into a friend personality for comfort. Whichever way works for you, you split a part of yourself within yourself that helps you control yourself.

That's it. The key step: make a "soul action figure" and split yourself from your soul.

There are a few key points to be made here.

One is, why do I say this is "splitting the self" to help control the self. This is mainly based on my own experience in practice to describe. Because of my severe domestic violence experience, as an adult, when the manager is particularly stressed, emotional outbursts are often fleeting, causing serious damage to my belongings and my own body. Later I thought about my course of action and found relief when there was another me in my mind comforting myself. Seeing this, I know what some readers want to say. Don't worry, I know what you're going to say, and I can only tell you that I have my right mind at all times, or I wouldn't be writing these words. This special state of mind is related to my childhood depression and autism, which is called introversion. That's not what I was born with, that's what I was brought up with, so a normal part of my personality is constantly trying to save itself. I always feel that I can't express myself properly in public, that I can't say anything interesting, and that I tend to get stuck in my head and be slow to speak. So I kept imagining those scenes in my mind, imagining what interesting things I could say and what wonderful expressions I could make in those scenes. Even if you confirm your suspicions, dear reader, I want to tell you that I have always been sane. I have never hurt anyone with my outbursts. I have always hurt myself. Don't worry, keep watching.

After experiencing this state of mind for a long time, I found a way to comfort myself, namely, my alter ego. He's not quite the same as the fantasy friend, he's not quite the same as the split personality, he's part of my own personality, I'm the same person. It's kind of like looking in a mirror, but not quite the same as looking in a mirror. The mirror is always doing the same thing as the real self, while the split inner self takes on part of my personality. He is me, but he only does the part that he takes on. It was very much like a "soul doll", where I made an inner version of myself and injected a part of my soul into it. This is a crucial step in using the "meeting with yourself" method.

Not only do you have to create the action figure and infuse it with soul, you also have to give it a name. For example, I used a pseudonym to name my soul doll. "Xing Guangyue" is my old self. He carries all kinds of memories and experiences of the past 30 years and is a gentle and calm subject soul."Gary Xing" is the new me. He carries the process of learning and exploration after I enter the new stage of life, and he is the relatively active subject soul."Lao Hai" is me with the character of the public. He is a magician, carrying my knowledge and memory of Buddhism, Zen, Taoism, Christianity and other religious fields. He is a friend's self. And "X" is a terrible guy, he carries all of my wild imagination, crazy impulses, extreme emotions and the desire to vent the petulant thoughts, this is the part I have to watch out for and have to suppress.

You may think this is perverted, a deliberate attempt to make yourself mentally ill. But do you remember what I mentioned in Method 9? The only thing a gangster fears more than anything else is being recognized by you. So, giving the evil part of you a name is the key to recognizing the evil in your soul. Of course, you also need to give a name to the gentle and kind part of your soul that you need to call upon to help you control demons at critical times, which I will refer to again later in "Exhaling the Name of the Angels."

You see, now we can begin our own exorcism rituals by having meetings with ourselves in "soul figures."

When I encounter some special situation, or the

mood of depression turns to irritability, I will suddenly realize that X has appeared. X is not another part of my personality, he is just a part of my soul, so I can take control of him and quickly call on the rest of my own "soul doll", constantly strengthening my main personality and bringing my other "soul dolls" together to help comfort and suppress this violent and evil part. The old sea will tell X, you still want to live, you can't do this, we still have hope, can try again, and so on.In this way, we can quickly and powerfully avoid emotional and behavioral loss of control and keep ourselves in our normal mind. In the eyes of others, you may be stunned or make some strange movements, but everything will be resolved in a second, and you will still be healthy and normal, and you will continue to live a healthy and normal life. If 1 second is not enough, try another second. They are in your heart and will definitely be at your disposal.

The second is the difference between this method and mental disorders. I think that's the most important thing you care about if you're planning to try this. All I can say is, they are different. Mental disorders are beyond your control, and this method always obeys your control. It's kind of like state of mind programming, where you write a program in advance to prevent a behavioral bug, and when a bug happens, the "soul doll" program launches quickly to fix it. You can make only one soul action figure, or you can make many, depending on what you like. I also liken this process to soul skin grafting. When we use skin grafts to treat patients with severe burns, the preferred skin is the patient's own skin to eliminate the risk of rejection. We make "soul puppets" within ourselves of this nature, naming parts of our souls, clearly recognizing their nature, and using them to suppress and soothe one another. In the critical moment when the bad emotions suddenly erupt, no matter who appears in your heart, they are you, you can control them, and there is no rejection reaction, so you are still healthy and normal, not abnormal mental. And that, I think, is the key difference.

The third is why such an outlandish approach is used. Remember the theme of the book? Our goal is to achieve psychological self-help in the state of major depression. If you've ever been in that depressive or manic state, you know what I'm talking about. But if you're not in that state and you can't understand what I'm saying, then you're healthy and normal and really don't need to use this method. It may seem odd, but there are already some similar methods, such as the "imaginary friend" often found in children, or the "stress bag" blown up in the heat of anger, all of which use an external object to help ease the mood. But why would I ignore those methods and suggest splitting myself and creating a "soul doll" in my own mind? Because, in my opinion, they're not powerful enough to ease your sudden surge of rage quickly and effectively when you need it. Although I have stressed many times that the "soul doll" is not a mental illness, bipolar disorder is a real mental illness, and the ferocity of its onset is not something that can be dealt with casually. Therefore, the use of such a method, completely belongs to their own soul to add a insurance, is the severe medicine for hard disease.

Method 14) Observe Your Life and Record It

Now I have a question for you: what was the title of the chapter you just read?

And the second question: How many times have you had a drink of water so far today?

Here's a third question: If you've seen a movie in the last month, just name one of them.

In fact, there are many problems, I will not go into details.

If you have all answered, congratulations, you are not only smart, but also healthy and lively.

If you can't answer any of them, don't worry. That's normal behavior for most people.

The questions I'm asking are the trivialities of life, which our memories temporarily store in our unconscious mind, where it helps to deal with them. The subconscious's way of dealing with these little things is to save them for a while and then throw them out when you dream at night so that your brain can get on with facing tomorrow, a new day, relaxed and happy.

So, if you are a very good memory, in addition to your gifts very well, or you're interested in training memory, or your opower is very big, a lot of people to butter you wait outside of these conditions, good memory probably because your heart some kind of damage, lead to abnormal development of memory, sometimes is lower, sometimes is enhanced. These changes are all part of the body's stress response to helping you through a crisis.

In fact, even if you think you have a bad memory and have forgotten a lot of things, your subconscious mind is actually storing a lot of memories for you to help you accumulate experience and cope with the bad events that may continue to come.

Our soul, our emotions, our feelings, and the way we act, are made up of these little things that are secretly remembered, without our dominant mind knowing it. It's our subconscious mind doing the work for us. Think about it. How many of the most important things that have happened in our lives so far? These events do affect our emotions, but for how long? And before these great events, are we all passionless and soulless?

Perhaps things are easier to understand if we use fitness as a metaphor. As we all know, fitness is a very perseverance test activity, fat metabolism is very difficult, only sustainable can be effective. If we continue jogging, or do some other aerobic exercise for 30 days, we will certainly feel lighter, but the actual weight change may not achieve the desired goal. If we continue to jog for 90 days, or even a year, then the effect becomes more pronounced. This is the cumulative effect of small changes. The structure of our soul, our emotional responses, our habits of behavior, are also built up in the small things that happen every day.

Unfortunately, our brains can't help us remember every little thing. It's a natural brain protective mechanism designed to keep us in a good mood every day. If you want to discover the secrets of your soul formation and transformation, you need to make a conscious effort to write down the little things that happen in your life every day.

In fact, we don't really know what little thing changed us, so not only do we need to write down the various things that happen to us each day, but we also need to pick up a journal and review it every once in a while. Just like keeping fit, when you keep this habit of observing your life and writing it down over a long period of time, you will discover many secrets about your life.

In this matter of recording life, do not be difficult to write in the form and level of literary classics. We are all ordinary people, the most common diary is ok, casually write down a sentence to record something happened today, there are a few things have a few words, this is enough.

You can also highlight your journal, use different colors, or draw some illustrations. Keeping it casual is the most important rule, which will make it easier to complete your journal. Start at any time, write at any time, keep it simple and clear, the better.

Perhaps you've heard of the book *Details Are the Devil*, which describes in great detail how to make things more successful by painting the perfect details. We observe our lives and write down the little things. All the little things are the details of our lives, and these details, indeed, make up the basic state of our lives and continue to influence our psychological state. We don't need to strive for perfection in these details, but we can change these details in the way we want to change our psychological state.

Once popular in Japan, the art of "unsheltered" objects arrangement, in essence, also changes our mentality and mood by changing the minuteness of our life, and gives us a relaxed attitude of life by using the empty living environment. Of course, it's not for everyone, like me. I like things to pile up. I find my sense of security in a mess of things in their place. Maybe there are a lot of people like me. We need to respect our choices and accept our mess without affecting others.

In his book Be a *Mentally Strong Woman: Carnegie's Book for the Spiritual Growth of Women*, Dale Carnegie (D.), the famous chicken soup master of the United States, also suggested to women: "...Use that time to read a book or two to improve your taste, and learn a little about literature, art, history, and culture."Personally, I don't like this argument, and I think Mr. Carnegie is just trying to convey the idea of "don't waste your time", but he does make an important point to all of us: all the little moments in our lives will add up and affect our lives now.

I forget who said that if all human beings kept records of their daily lives, the history of mankind would not be what it is today, but would be more sincere, more civilized and more developed. Very regrettably, I searched repeatedly but failed to find the source of this sentence. If I had recorded it at that time, I would not have such a regret today.

For your own good mood, and for the sake of human civilization, observe your life today and write it down.

Method 15) Find Your interest

I know very well what it's like to have a bout of depression, and loss of interest is one of the main states of depression. As far as I am concerned, the state when I have interest and the state when I lose interest are very significant. My psychological feelings are clear and obvious.

In peacetime, I like handmade, including making simple furniture, making wooden toys, or refitting small electrical appliances and so on. I don't usually make things by hand, but when I'm not making anything, I think and imagine in my head what my next craft will be. But, if the depression attack, I will really feel that all this is so boring, meaningless, more not fun, the brain is completely no spark of imagination, it is really a dark.

At this point, you might say, if you have clear interests but still can't resist a bout of depression, why introduce us to the useless business of "finding interests"?

I really need to say something about that, because I've thought a lot about the question that you might ask.

I think this is due to the limited amount of effort I put into my hobbies and the fact that my hobbies don't give me much feedback. Here are five things I've found that might make your hobby interesting enough to fight off depression.

1• A specific interest may be better than a broad interest. There are many things in life that can be hobbies, such as collecting stamps, collecting bottle caps, carving, and certain skills, and so on. In my childhood, everybody is very happy to stamp collecting, like Mr. Huxley said in his works "*Brave New World*", the differentiation from embryonic period manufacture industry workers to their standard of fun, let them in the busy hard work, can the mind be some relaxing place, so that they don't make things easily. The equivalent of stamp collecting is collecting cigarette and match boxes, collecting bottle caps, sweet wrappers, and so on. Collecting is of the most widespread interest. There is even a shop in Taiwan, willing to collect all kinds of instant noodles from all over the world, as long as they are different, all collect, and with this as the theme of the World Instant Noodles shop, very novel. In addition, there are skills of interest, such as I once read a news in a local newspaper, said that a primary school students walk to and from school, because of boredom, so with his fingers touching the iron railings along the way, after a long time, actually practiced into a powerful invincible one finger Zen, and to repel the little rascals.

People are happy to invest in their skills and constantly experience the pleasure of their growing strength, which is different from the form of collecting objects, but the essence is similar. The so-called interest, is that people will feel happy and interesting, in various forms, essentially is to invest their own energy, and let oneself feel stronger, richer, richer fun, that is, to get the pleasure of self-motivation.

People's energy has its limits, interests are wide, energy is scattered, interest is relatively specific, energy is concentrated. When you're focused, you'll get better results, and you'll feel more self-motivated. Originally, interest is a very personalized thing, and there is no difference between specificity and broad. However, for depressed patients, a relatively broad interest may not be as effective as a relatively specific interest in eliciting self-motivated pleasure, so the effect of interest in improving depression will appear to be less.

2• Interest closely connected with reality can obtain more social incentives. Taking the above example as an example, it seems more practical to collect cigarette boxes, match boxes and sweet wrappers than to collect different flavors of instant noodles from all over the world and set up a shop to sell them. In practice, I mean in terms of making money.

All good social incentives are often carried by money. Just like painting art, painting very well, naturally can earn a lot of money, if you can't earn a lot of money, that is, of course, painting is not good. Vincent Willem van Gogh's paintings are priceless today, because today people think he painted so well. Only one of Mr. Van Gogh's 2,000-odd paintings, "The Red Vineyard", was bought by his brother, Theodorus Van Gogh, for 400 francs (about $1,000 today), 15 months after it was made. Mr. Vincent did not know about it and it is the only painting by Vincent Van Gogh that was ever sold. No one wanted to buy Mr. Van Gogh's paintings because they were considered eccentric and out of the mainstream, and no great work was worth it. This is a sign of The Times, but also Mr. Vincent's personal tragedy and helplessness.

We can choose to be a successful art dealer walking in the bustling world like Mr. Theo, or we can choose to be a tragic genius surpassing the mundane world like Mr. Van Gogh. Of course, we should choose to be ourselves. Fun is the point, money is not money, is not important. But maybe it would be more fun if we could make some money.

3. Interest that can enhance personal strength can obtain more self-motivation. In fact, among the optional interests, there is indeed some kind of project, such as kung fu, that allows both personal and social incentives to exist together. When we begin to practice kungfu and get past the initial painful period of laying the foundation, the happiness of growth immediately follows. Every day of training can let oneself experience the pleasure of upgrading, and the pleasure of constantly getting stronger is filled with the whole body. When kung fu practice is small enough to take part in some competitions, we begin to integrate with the secular world. Kung fu continues to improve, and as we achieve success and victory, personal interest and worldly success will follow. Mr. Bruce Lee is one of the most representative figures. If practice is quite good also, do not want to take the road of challenge stage however, so go making movie actor is very good also, the dragon tiger martial arts division of Hong Kong 1980 time, monthly salary can reach 5000 Hong Kong dollars or so, although very hard, but also fame and fortune receive. This kind of interest is really enviable.

Similarly, there are many other interests, such as painting as mentioned above, music skills, wood carving, fitness, etc. Any interest that can continuously improve your own strength, including hairstyle making, makeup skills, etc., is also a great interest. From this perspective, interest is more like an evolutionary state of childhood "play," which is preparatory work to acquire survival skills.

Children like to play, because free play makes them happy. Interest also has the same property. It is more important to make themselves happy before truly acquiring certain survival skills. Learning a skill that doesn't motivate you or make you happy, and then taking a job you hate, is probably the last thing you have to do. If things go on like this, even a healthy mind will fall into depression.

4• The best interest is a lifelong interest. Some interest to do for a long time, most of their life into it, so this interest has a sense of dependence. Just as people who have been doctors all their lives always want to get up early to make rounds, older drivers who are used to driving buses are used to taking bus routes even when they walk. If you can find a hobby that you can happily devote a lot of energy to, and to which you can build your skills and strengths, then you are indeed lucky. Be sure to cherish this happiness.

I once heard such a story: An old woman wanted to learn to play the piano. This was one of her dreams when she was young, but at the age of 70, she was afraid that she was too old and would die before she could learn to play, so she just thought about it and gave up. As a result, she lived to the age of 80, still in excellent health. She remembered her dream of learning to play the piano 10 years ago and lamented that if she had started learning at the age of 70, she would have played the piano for 10 years now and would have been able to play Mr. Ludwig van Beethoven's compositions smoothly.

The opposite motivational story exists in the real world, so look it up for yourself. If this is your hobby, it's never too late to start.

Writing is one of my interests. I am the kind of person with many interests and miscellaneous, so that the shallow energy was divided very much, and I failed to form a deep accumulation in a certain interest, which is my regret. I will concentrate on accumulating and training my writing skills from now on, and I hope this interest will be with me for the rest of my life.

Find the one interest that will last your whole life. When you find it, don't forget to hold on.

5• Finally, are your interests enough to relax you? After all, the starting point of interest is not survival, but something beyond survival, its essence is pleasure, and this pleasure belongs to your soul. So, whatever your interest, ask yourself, is this fun enough to make you happy? For example, if your hobby is running, running will be very tiring, but after running, you will feel relaxed, cheerful and energetic, then it is really a good hobby. Then you can answer the question by saying, "Yes, I'm happy."

Then ask yourself, is this interest fulfilling enough for you? Let's say you're interested in carpentry. It's very tiring to move wood, and then you have to do tedious, even painstakingly fine processing.

But when the woodworking is done, you see your work there, a unique creation, born of your imagination and your hands. What do you say at this point? Yes, it enriches me.

Then ask yourself, is this interest relaxing enough? Let's say your interest, like mine, is writing. You must have experienced something extremely depressing, something simmering in the back of your mind that is difficult to release, your characters and story hidden in a corner of your mind, but you can't find them anyway. It was more painful than not being able to poop. And when you finally catch them and begin to write a story that is yours and theirs, thousands of miles, hundreds of years, and when the story is over, the night outside the window is black and the hair and hair on your face are white, and you feel as if you have experienced so much time at the same time that you have forgotten the present moment. Are you also like me, feel that relaxed?

Actually, I would say, don't pay too much attention to the above three questions. For me, just being able to answer one of these questions is already a good interest. If one does not answer, that also does not count as nothing, as long as oneself like, that is the most important.

Okay, that's the end of this title. I need to say again that interest is a very important thing, just like a partner with a gentle personality who loves to talk and laugh. If before 40 years old, we have to rely on the passion of struggle to support life, then after 40 years old, probably will rely on interest to adjust life. Life without interest is like a steak without sauce. It is fresh but tasteless.

Go find your interest, as long as not dead, everything is not too late.

Method 16) Keep Reading

Books are an important support for the development of human civilization. The overall reading volume of a nation is an important index to measure the level of civilization of a nation.

However, when the reading scale of a nation or an individual shows a continuous growth trend, we still cannot be optimistic. During this period, we observe what they are reading. It's like when the adolescent body is developing, the amount of food they eat increases significantly, and we need to pay attention to what they are eating during this process. Are they completely high in salt, sugar and fat, or do they follow a balanced diet of meat, vegetables, eggs and milk? When we eat, we pay more attention to healthy choices. When we read, we need to focus on comprehensive and balanced healthy reading habits.

At the beginning of reading, about will be affected by the education level, reading will be relatively slow, often need to look up the dictionary, learn words. When the amount of reading accumulated to a certain extent, the reading speed will be significantly improved. Everyone is different, so there is no such thing as "standard reading", you just need to "keep reading".

Improving your reading speed does not mean

reading every word of a book once and reading the whole thing. You can do this with the words you like, or the accepted classics, and it's worth it, even if it's a slow read. If a book is in your hands and you don't feel that it has any special value, then it's perfectly fine to speed read in this way, taking in the general idea of the text, and just getting the direction and atmosphere of the text.

The more experience you have in reading, the more likely you will appreciate the different styles of different authors. These styles are often so different that you must be sensitive to the fact that you seem to love one author's style and deeply dislike the other's oddities. My personal advice to this is: it's normal to be picky, but don't go overboard. Excessive picky food, may cause your mental malnutrition. Chances are you'll get into a habit of reading a certain type or style and discard most of the rest. This will limit your reading boundaries, that is, your thinking boundaries. Sometimes this restriction comes from the outside world, and more often it comes from within yourself. You might think reading Calvino would be so cool that you'd forgo Stephen King and Poe, Andersen and the Brothers Grimm, and even Shakespeare would be relegated to the shelf as an old fable. When you think about it, how much great wisdom did you miss?

We do not know which snowflake caused the avalanche, so we do not know which book, article, or sentence opened the door of our wisdom. Therefore, it is very necessary to keep reading.

If nurtured fastidious and biased reading habit, this is really a very regrettable thing. But it's still a hundred times better than reading stupidly.

What is reading stupidly? Here are five points.

1• Reading harmful books without knowing it. Just as there are poisonous foods, there are also poisonous books. But just as it is difficult for humans to identify poisonous mushrooms, it is even more difficult to identify poisonous books. There was a book called "*Water Knows the Answer*" that came out of nowhere in 1999 and took Asia by storm at the beginning of the 21st century. But as we know today, it was pseudoscience and a hoax. Similar scams are still everywhere today. Moreover, in the field of books, human beings often have an inexplicable opposite judgment between "good" and "bad," with "good" being considered "bad" and "bad" being considered "good. Mr. James Augustine Aloysius Joyce's masterpiece "*Ulysses*" was rejected more than a dozen times before it was published, and Mr. Nabokov's "*Lolita*" was similarly rejected. The aforementioned book, Lady Chatterley's Lover, went through a similar tortuous journey. Reading this far, you might think that my reading habits seem to be particularly weighted toward a particular kind of literature. Congratulations, you guessed it, but not in that category, but in the horror category. If you've ever read about mainstream literary attitudes toward horror king Stephen King before he was awarded the National Book Award for Lifetime Achievement in 2003, you might agree with me. In contrast, the name of the banner of nostalgia to carry forward the ignorant and backward books, for the emperor's hymns of the books are popular. Perhaps the only way we can combat harmful books is to detoxify the harmful books we accidentally read by constantly increasing our reading, by continuously, widely, and comprehensively reading all kinds of books and all styles of books. If you read extensively enough and think independently enough, I believe you can tell at a glance which books are poisonous.

2• Read and only read books by political ICONS. This is the stupidest way to read. None of them.

3• Indulge in ancient books. Ancient books are a good thing, especially literature and art, which can let our thoughts travel through time and space and enjoy the glory of the old moon. But it would be unwise to dwell on it. In essence, ancient books are not different from books of today. They are books, just older, with the old-fashioned style of writing, that's all. Because of the love of ancient books, there is an atmosphere of everything being ancient, which is really bad. So like the old things, why not always hold their own kindergarten written words, painting to study seriously?

4• Indefatigably nibbling away at books. Not every book needs to be read from cover to cover. You don't have to memorize exactly what each chapter tells you. You don't need to fully understand the exact meaning of every word. Not every sentence has a metaphor. Not every paragraph has a general idea. Not every article can be divided into sections and summarized. All the reading in the world with standard answers is meant to make you dumber, not smarter.

5• Believe everything in the book. If you've done what I said in the last paragraph, then you can ignore what I'm going to say in this paragraph. If you don't understand what I said in the last paragraph, then you will inevitably follow the title of this paragraph. Maybe not in this book, but you're bound to fall into it.

Reading is a slow-burning pastime, and learning from books is only a bonus to the act of reading. In addition to knowledge, constant reading can help us expand our minds, keep fresh input, keep our soul alive, unconsciously strengthen our spirit, stimulate brainstorming, and help depressed people gradually restore their creativity.

But under Gutenberg's starry skies, is it the great Bible or pornography that has spread more? That's a problem.

Method 17) Vipassana Self: Call Upon the Name of Angel

This is the opposite of Method 9, when we want to fight the devil, we need to know its name, know what it is, and then we can target it.

And when we want to receive the kind things and feel the love, we also need to recognize the names of angels, so that when they appear in front of us, we will not know that God's angels have come.

Perhaps the name of the greatest angel for people suffering from depression should be "understanding," the kind of understanding that is empathy. This world is the most not lack of reason, random nonsense can also make up 100 million reasons to comfort others, but few people can sincerely stand in the other side of the Angle to think about. If someone does, he must be your angel.

Again, though, we need to think about this a little more rigorously.

For example, when you are disappointed in a romantic relationship, or when an investment goes bad, or when you lose a significant family member, you feel depressed and can't help it. Then a friend of yours shows up who has been through the same thing, and you know she has been through the same thing, and the words of comfort will be very close to your heart, because your pain and depression will be much easier to ease because you have shared the same painful experience. Poet Mr. Gu Cheng has a poem entitled "Wu", the content of the poem is: gum like/slowly shed tears/glue to the heart fragments/make us fall in love/common pain/not revelry. It is this state of "understanding" that is described. The advantage of this method is obvious, because it is close to the heart that you need to soothe.

On the other hand, if someone tries to soothe you in the usual way and tries to soothe you in his own way, does that mean "not understanding" you? In my opinion, if someone appears as a mentor, under the banner of the road of life to your soul chicken soup type persuasion, this kind of situation is nine out of ten hypocrites in cheating money. But if your family and friends do this, they're probably just following the same rules that everyone else uses, and that's fine. It's very important to understand that, because most people in this world are not experts in psychology, and they are not experts in persuasion. They have to do it the way they understand it, which is also a sign of kindness. And best of all, this method, which complies with the aforementioned principle of "diversity," can actually save your life. Maybe they meant well and didn't tell you what you wanted to hear, but you gained fresh information that helped your mind and heart find new ways.

When a relative or friend goes their own way, there are only two things you need to avoid and you have a good chance of reversing your depression. One is that the consoler keeps saying nasty and disgusting things under the guise of comforting you, which is called "the knife's bite is worse than the heart's bite". Trust me, that's not kindness, that's perversion. The second is your own big baby mentality. Do not think that this world only you wronged, also do not think that you wronged can do whatever you want. As a normal life, it is normal to be wronged and injured. It is not a big deal. It serves you right not to be able to accept genuinely well-meaning offers of advice that you don't think the same way just because you're hurt. Depression can be painful, but it's not a big deal. Don't take yourself too seriously. It will help you recover.

Say that finish others, we also need to say back to yourself. If we are cognizant of the goodwill of others, why do we need to see the inner self? This is very important. If the kindness of others is like a ship, then your heart is the harbor where these ships dock.

When you long for love, you also need to ask yourself first, do you have this love in your heart?

While you long for understanding and compassion from within, you need to first ask yourself if there is genuine understanding and compassion within you as well.

If you don't have these angels' harbors in your heart, how can you expect others' ships of goodwill to dock?

You need to give the desired kindness a name, such as "love", such as "care", or some other name you can understand and accept. Call them to your heart when you need them, and take the first steps to spread that kindness to the people around you. You need the angel of goodwill, others also need, even if you are depressed patients, also can't like a child wanton demand, capricious.

Here, I want to help you identify one more devil, whose form is as follows.

If you feel sorry for yourself, bemoan your depression and pain, but never care about what others think or feel, or extend the kind acts of kindness you wish to receive, I can only tell you that this behavior is called selfishness. This is what "selfish" demons look like.

A person with this selfish attribute cannot feel the kindness of others, no matter how kind they are to him, because his selfishness prevents him from distinguishing good from evil. And this depression, full of selfishness, is no consolation.

If you want to find comfort, start by exhaling the name of an angel.

Have a joke, here share with you: the flood happened somewhere, a man in the water prayer god's help, at this moment, a boat rowed to a raft the people on the raft tried to seize him, but this person to escape, and Shouting at the people on the raft, says he is a devout believers, only waiting for god's help, so the raft and left. Before long, a lifeboat came, the people in the boat tried to save him, but he also scolded away. When the third rescue boat was also chased away by him, he finally lost his strength and drowned. At the intersection of heaven and hell, his ghost met God and asked God: I believe in you so devoutly, why don't you save me? God is very helpless to say: I have sent an angel respectively driving 3 boats to save you, but you drive away, how could I do with that?

At the intersection of heaven and hell, where will this man go?

Method 18) Think About the Universe

The act of thinking about the universe always brings me the most imagination space and thinking inspiration. Like the strike of a match, the spark leaped uncontrollably.

So, what do we need to think about the universe? For me, there is no fixed direction, but I can start from the following aspects one by one. Readers can do as they please and follow the direction they like. In any case, from the point of view of depression relief, we think about the universe for the purpose of relaxation and relief, not for the purpose of scientific research, so we don't have to worry too much about the precision of the data and the theoretical basis that is still considered correct in our time.

From this point of view, I will only make the simplest concept introduction here, and give you the key words, the depth of thinking is entirely up to your personal preference.

"Redshift". The strong supporting evidence of the cosmic inflation theory is an important observation data for the study of the big bang and the boundary of the universe. The universe we live in was born out of the original Singularity Big Bang, right? The force of the explosion has not stopped, so the universe is still expanding? So we can figure out the boundary of the universe? So what does the boundary of the universe look like? What does it look like beyond the boundaries of the universe? If the Big Bang was like lighting a match, was the universe, which we perceive as almost eternal, just a flash of light in some other world?

"Stars from hundreds of millions of years ago". To think about this keyword, we first need to know a few concepts and their data. The speed of light, which refers to the speed of light in a vacuum, is a physical constant, commonly referred to as C, with an exact value of 299,792458m /s (sometimes 3.00×108 m/s).Light-year, a unit of length, refers to the distance that light travels in one year in a vacuum, which is approximately 9.46 trillion kilometers (9.46×1012 kilometers or 5.88×1012 miles).It takes about 8 minutes and 20 seconds for light to travel from the Sun to the Earth, which means that the light we see from the Sun is the light that left the Sun's surface 8 minutes and 20 seconds ago. The closest star to the Sun, Proxima Centauri, is about 4.243 light-years from Earth, which means that when we observe the star from Earth, we see light that departed from Proxima Centauri four years and three months ago.MACS0677-JD is a likely candidate for the farthest galaxy ever observed. It has a redshift of z=10.7, or about 13.3 billion light-years from Earth. When we look at this galaxy from Earth, we see light that started out from that galaxy 13.3 billion years ago. From this point of view, when we find a star that is so bright, maybe that star is just the last light that was emitted when that star exploded tens of millions of years ago. The human visual world is carried by light. The human brain can interpret the light scattering information, but perhaps because of the lack of precision, we can't interpret the dense light that reaches our eyes. This is like the VCD machine reading laser head can not read the DVD disc data like that. Our brains are powerless against the light that has traveled through the universe for billions of light-years. Even the light of the sun cannot be accurately interpreted by our eyes and our brains. But if, one day, we could rely on sophisticated machines to decipher the light, what secrets might we find in it? And what if, one day, we captured all the light that has been scattering out of the Earth in the universe for 4.6 billion years? What would we see in "Earthlight"?At that time, having possessed such advanced civilization and technology, could human beings be sincere and calm in the face of these ancient but vivid stories?

"Double slit experiment". Double slit experiment, or double slit experiment, is an experiment to demonstrate the wave and particle properties of microscopic objects such as photons or electrons. The experiment itself is quite interesting, but as the process is complex, I ask you to check the details for yourself. The experiment was so interesting that quantum physicists dubbed it the "Copenhagen Interpretation," but at the same time there were people kicking through the fence and a related thought experiment known as Schrodinger's Cat. There are also "Quantum Eraser Experiment" and "Wheeler's Delayed Choice Experiment" and other very wonderful experiments on quantum states. They are too complex and professional, so please check them out on your own based on your interest. It's definitely worth it. Scientists' observations of quantum states have made our physical world so confusing that we think of the antecedent and the consequent really are? Does time flow in positive order as we perceive it? Do multiuniverses, parallel universes, sliced-universes, which exist only in thought experiments, really exist?

Thinking, and enjoy it.

Method 19) Go and Feel Nature

There are a lot of amazing things in nature, and if your soul is stuck deep inside you, maybe a touch of green in nature can help you get back into the big, sunny world.

With the development and expansion of the

world economy, the urban steel jungle gradually encroach on the natural forest full of green vitality. In terms of distance from Tokyo, a world-class international metropolis, the urban scenery of Tokyo in reality is even like the futuristic sci-fi city in Ghost in the Shell, where endless prosperity covers up the huge pressure in people's hearts, and economic prosperity whiteshoes people's fatigued and excessive expression. But we still hear about Tokyo's special epithet, "City of Depression," and the unavoidably high suicide rate.

When you're feeling depressed or in a stressful situation, it's time to get in touch with nature. There are many ways you can choose, such as going to the window to breathe the fresh air, looking at the distant blue sky, walking on the street, looking for a park, observing a flower, walking barefoot on the lawn, observing ants or other insects, listening to birds, and so on.

If you find a small river or stream, you can also try, if it's safe to do so, throwing a handful of water and sprinkling it all around.

When it rains, try to walk on the road without an umbrella. An umbrella or a raincoat will increase the tension of avoiding the rain in your heart, and abandoning those defenses will give you a sense of relief. It's not necessary, of course, but it's worth trying, and maybe you'll get some of the joy you get from Singin' in the Rain.

If, for some reason, none of the above is easy for you to do, there are some alternatives to try. Pick up a twig, a leaf, or a dandelion flower on the ground, and observe it when you can be alone. Look at the texture of its skin, the hairs, the veins, the color, and smell it. Look as closely as you can. You are bound to discover something about nature, or yourself, that you did not know before, and experience a certain mysterious beauty in it. This approach is well worth trying, not only as a way of relieving depression, but also as a way of feeling, thinking and writing. I was a poet before I became a horror writer. At that time I had not yet found a cure for depression, so the poet did not pass through the pain of depression, and it had almost dissipated. I hardly ever write poetry anymore, though I can still use verse. If the beauty and suffering of nature and life are not sincerely displayed, no matter how clever those rhymes, they are no different from children's songs.

In addition, we can also try to cultivate plants, fish and so on, to bring the breath of nature to our side. However, I personally don't recommend keeping pets like cats or dogs when you are depressed. People may see this by different way, but all up to you.

Human beings are also one of the creations of nature. Comparing the earth to the mother, comparing the nature to the mother. When our mood is in a bad state of depression, returning to the embrace of the mother, we can always return to the carefree childhood.

Method 20) Faith: Six Paramitas

"Six Paramitas" is a special term in Buddhism,

also known as "Six Ways to Cultivate Tao", which refers to the moral qualities of the six Bodhisattva practices, namely "giving, keeping precepts, forbear insults, pursuit, meditation, and wisdom". It is believed that if one can practice six degrees steadfastly, one can overcome the sea of life and death distress. Reaching the shore of Nirvana. I was a Buddhist before I was a Christian, and of course I became a Taoist after a long time, and then a long time before I finally became a Christian. I did not have a special initiation ritual in any of my beliefs, that is, as a Buddhist, I did not receive a ordination. When I was a Taoist, I never worshiped a teacher. When I was a Christian, I was never baptized.

I don't like the rules of each religion, and I don't like the tradition of "preaching on behalf of God."My spiritual core is fundamentalist, my way of behaving is Protestant. All these, I think, have not affected my heartfelt respect and faith for God and God.

As a Buddhist, I recognized my inborn Buddha as Avalokitasvara because I was inspired by The Si-

Syllable Mantra, which means Oṃ mamani Padme H,

and I continued to practice them on this page. I also studied the mantras of other Bodhisattvas, and of course I studied the relevant books carefully. Later, with the deepening understanding of the technology of "six lines prediction", I developed a strong interest in Taoism, and learned the incantations such as "Taoist Existence Mantra" independently, as well as the techniques of painting and prediction. I later converted to Christianity because of my love of the Lord's Prayer. If there is a chance in the future, perhaps I will become a believer of another denomination, and God will show me the way.

I highly recommend religious practice if you are focused on spiritual cultivation and not so much on the influence of religion on the world. You can choose any religion that suits you, learn about it, understand it, and commit to it. Each religion is unique in terms of the cultivation of the individual soul. Throwing away all the worldly judgments of "good" and "evil" and simply doing a spiritual exercise, perhaps you will find a home for your soul in religion.

Don't know how many people is because of the diamond sutra, "all the promising method, such as illusory, like dew or like electricity, should be done that way" and "born should not live their heart" this two sentences and suddenly enlightened, and how many people because of the six ancestors altar sutra "is not is pneumatic, discussion, cardiac" such sentences and stories, when your soul depressed and helpless, I am sure you will find a place for your own soul in the religious texts.

What we're talking about is just about yourself, about your own soul. Preachers on behalf of the Lord, their ways are many false; the righteousness of those who do what is right on behalf of the Lord will be evil. When the world is false and evil, it always likes to pull a big flag to be its FIG leaf, which is really filthy and stinking.

It is enough to find a faith in one's heart, to find a way of salvation for one's soul, not to use the name of God to decorate one's good deeds, and not to use the name of God to cover one's evil deeds.

Ⅳ·Reading Recommendation

The readings in this recommended list are not in any particular order, nor do they have any particular meaning, nor are they even arranged alphabetically by last name, nor even by rank of fame. That means you can choose to read some of them, all of them, or none at all. You don't need to suffer from any kind of pressure like perfectionism, and you definitely don't need to suffer from any psychological burden. The recommended book is also a complete mess of logic, and if you can't find something hidden, that's perfectly normal. It's not your problem.

As we have explained the function of reading in the previous article, it is up to you to decide what to read. Of course, it doesn't matter at all if you don't read any. It's a very common choice, and it's perfectly normal.

1·*The Man in the High Castle*, Philip Kindred Dick
2·*Brave New World*, Aldous Leonard Huxley
3·*Mini Habits*, Stephen Guise
4·*Kiraware Matsuko no isshô*, Yamada Muneki
5·*Toxic Parents: Overcoming Their Hurtful Legacy and Reclaiming Your Life*, Susan Forward / Craig Buck
6·*Danshari: Shin Katazukejutsu*, Yamashita Hideko
7·*The Little Prince*, Antoine de Saint-Exupéry
8·*Namiya Zakkaten no Kiseki*, Higashino Keigo
9·*No Longer Human*, Dazai Osamu
10·*Hard-Boiled Wonderland and the End of the*

World, Murakami Haruki

Postscript: Reflections on the Soul

Thank you very much for reading this far.

This is not a popular science book, but it's not fantasy either, if you have to find a better metaphor, it's probably a self-report by a human rat. That is, as a former major depressive patient, I write a report of my feelings.

When I was young, I had read an interesting story about scientists, about a scientist for drug hallucinogenic have intense curiosity, so trying, toxicity attack for the first time, he experienced unparalleled joy, and saw the truth, in this happy but it's a pity that he failed to record was unconscious, wake up after the truth has been forgotten. Then, with a pen and paper at hand, he tried a second time, and in a blaze of vision he saw the truth again, and tried his best to write it down before he fainted. When he woke up, he immediately checked the note on the paper. It was scrawled in scrawled handwriting: "The banana is big, but the banana skin is bigger."That's probably the property of my book.

I don't know whether the book have any value, but because I have been suffering from depression, knew where the disease of the disaster, and accidentally got a suitable for my own self relief way, this a series of process, let me feel some kind of god's will, let me think it should be the will of god, complete self-help guide me, And to use my modest efforts to help other people in need of such help. In reality, there are more than 10 feelings of depression. I think everyone has different feelings, and there are not only 20 ways to relieve depression. I believe it should be endless, as long as we are still trying to live, we will always find some new ways.

People who do not know depression, it is difficult to know its harm. People who suffer from depression rarely have written words to describe their pain. I think I know why. Though I can save his life, but in my symptoms, painful sitting in front of the desk, I can only think of their useless, think about your own words is meaningless, and thinking about what you could finish, even if only to write a word, also can let me feel very terrorist and force can't win, don't see the future, no hope. In short, I couldn't write anything as long as I was sick. But this is what made me decide to write these words when I was in a right mood, so that more people would know and understand this terrible state of affairs.

It is a matter of great importance to the human soul.

If a person is suffering from physical pain and bleeding, people will often sympathize and try to help. But patients with depression are bleeding in the heart, the soul is broken, suffering unspeakably, and the body is not a big problem, even can smile, they should not get sympathy and treatment? We are the same people, the pain in the soul more need comfort.

In particular, people with depression rarely show aggressive behavior, which means they are poor people with broken souls, and sometimes a soft word or two can pull them back from the brink. Why not?

I'm not going to give you the numbers here, but

you can go online and look up the global incidence of depression and so on, and you can find them very easily. And because of the special nature of depression, my personal estimate is that the actual number of depression cases in the world may more than double, because a lot of people may just think they are in a bad mood, or in a bad mood, but never think they have this disease. Even if they do, they probably won't go to the hospital, as I describe in my book, for some reason, at least I haven't been to the hospital. So it's hard to imagine how many people suffer from depression. One prominent health organization even predicts that depression may become the second leading cause of human disease after heart disease by 2020, which is 2021, but this figure is still hard to verify. In a word, the suffering of the human soul is a terrible trouble.

Here, again, I quote a Wikipedia description of "depression": "Depression tends to heal well under aggressive treatment, but considering the extreme suffering and the risk of suicide, aggressive treatment should be initiated as soon as possible."Patients are likely to relapse after symptom remission, and the World Health Organization recommends drug treatment for depression continue until at least six months after symptom remission. For patients with earlier onset, psychotic symptoms or adverse drug reactions, it is likely to have repeated attacks resulting in adverse consequences.(Extract from Wikipedia entry "Depression" : same link as before.) This description also reminds us that the fight against depression requires people's sustained efforts and joint persistence.

In the process of writing this book, my heart kept producing "meaningless" this kind of desperate hiss, I do not know whether the writing of this book is meaningful or not, I am good or not, I even ask myself "meaning this thing is what the fuck."But I was also constantly, trying to think: what the hell, this is my world, I'm just trying to help people, I'm just trying to do what I love, I'm not hurting anyone, it's meaningless, it's all fart, as long as I like it.So I finished the book in the midst of this intense psychological conflict and conflict. I think, this is my self-help behavior. In this case, at least, I managed to save myself.

Each of us is a unique individual, and the world may have shaped us that way for a unique purpose that we are not aware of.

The world is tough, and we all have to deal with it. No one can get an "exemption from all diseases," so let's learn, discover, and confront this hateful disease together.

When our souls are brave enough to redeem themselves, perhaps we have acquired some special power to help others.

And when we try to help others, we may also be helping ourselves.

Thank you.

Finally, I want to thank my wife Lucy,
She didn't mind me staying home every day to write a book instead of going out to earn money.
I also want to thank Mr. Knickallan Adrian Zhou, who is a friend of mine,
In my most absurd and painful moments, he always called to comfort me.
And thank you to all who remember me,
Thank you.

Editor: Guangyue Xing

Cover design: Gary Xing

Remember the beginning of this book

About "The ultimate self help"?

The person you truly trust.

Maybe it's just yourself.